Backpacking Through Divorce

How to Deal when you've been Ditched

By Sean Hinchey

www.BackpackingThroughDivorce.com

Published by Liquid Footprint Publishing
PO Box 1977
Venice CA 90294

Printed in Canada

Diagrams by Bryan Swoboda of Glaucus Productions

Cover by Richard Black

Library of Congress Cataloging-in-Publication Data

Hinchey, Sean
Backpacking Through Divorce: How To Deal When You've Been Ditched.
1st Edition

ISBN: 0-9763595-051995

1. Self-Help
2. Divorce
3. Recovery
4. Relationships

TABLE OF CONTENTS

ACKNOWLEDGEMENTS

I couldn't have undertaken this task without so many people to help me.

Thanks to Bryan for taking my incoherent thoughts and turning them into remarkable diagrams, and for allowing me to set up camp on his couch on numerous occasions.

To Scott, for coming up with the title.

To Rick and KC for keeping me gainfully employed, and thanks to every other low-life I've had the privilege of working with in the mad cap world of AV Staging. Your breed never gave up on me, even when I had my doubts.

To Mrs. Ward, Dr. Welch and the late Mr. Sepe and Mrs. Lewis for being the most influential teachers to grace the earth.

To Lana for her compassion.

To my family.

To the men and women in all branches of the US Armed Services. Their fight to protect our freedoms has allowed me the luxury of writing this book.

NOTE TO THE READER

Men have a different way of coping with problems than their counterparts. In general, women look at things in a more emotional sense, whereas men tend to logically take things apart to see how they work. In doing so, they are capable of putting it back together so that it will work in a more fluid manner.

However, looking at one's life when the tragedy of a divorce occurs takes more focus than just disassembling the marriage. It takes a lot of thought and acceptance of responsibility. The emotional component cannot be overlooked.

After just over five years of marriage, I found out that it was over. No build up, no warning signs. Just finality.

Countless questions welled up inside me. Emotions such as hate, anger and rejection filled my soul. I didn't want to face the ugly truths that life had presented to me. But I did. In the process, I learned a great deal about myself.

For better or worse, it was a new opportunity. Only by diving head first into the problem was I able to cope with the fact that my marriage was over – completely against my wishes.

This book is written for the man who has been left behind by his wife - or girlfriend - and doesn't know what to do. I've been there, and it's not a happy place to be.

DISCLAIMER

The book is meant to assist you with coping with your divorce. It is not intended to discourage or hinder you from seeking the expertise of a lawyer, accountant, doctor, or other professional. The author will not accept any responsibility for any loss or damage caused directly or indirectly by the contents of this book.

If you do not wish to be bound by the above, contact the publisher for a full refund.

1

SITUATION: GRIM

WHO AM I?

That's best answered by telling you who I'm not. I don't have a PhD, nor do I run a marriage counseling practice with years of research compiled into one concise book. I have no formal training in any aspect of analysis or therapy. I haven't published any books on this subject, nor do I have a radio talk show. So what makes me capable of writing such a book?

Simply this, life experience. I'm giving you an outline of what I went through and how I managed to get myself back on course. I'll let the experts critique my credentials.

Before we embark on this journey, let me set the stage. You've been dropped into a forest – high trees block the sunlight trying to reach the ground. Scary noises of unseen creatures chill your bones.

But somewhere out there is hope. It's calling to you, imploring you to move forward. Hope can get you out of the woods. The quest is yours alone. What I have to share with you may help, or it may be meaningless gibberish.

There's a saying that goes, "The journey of a thousand miles begins with a single step." Profound. But it doesn't tackle the problem of the million or so steps that follow that first one.

The quest is yours alone.

When I was hit with the divorce, I flipped out. After moving out of the house and putting everything I owned into storage, I took off to Europe for three weeks. During that time, I kept a detailed journal in the form of a computer blog and managed to put my life back together. I want to tell you how I did, and elaborate on what worked for me.

I'm not suggesting that this book should replace any sort of therapy. That is a decision that you need to make. I look at this book as another means to aid in your healing process.

I don't bring up the topic of children in this book. Having no children of my own, I don't know how my divorce would've affected them. So, I didn't attempt to write about what I didn't experience firsthand.

This book is about you getting through some of the pain and chaos that a divorce has brought into your life.

If you can't get your own life in order, what good are you to your children?

THE CHALLENGE

I've got a proposition for you. If you put your first foot forward, you my find that the next step will be easier.

The journey will be hard, sometimes tortuous; yes it'll suck, but you won't die. The only way out of this forest is to go through it. There's no shortcut, no wandering around the perimeter.

There's no shortcut, no wandering around the perimeter.

So, the more time you spend wandering around in the same circle, burning a hole in the ground, the less time you have to move on and get on with your life.

In life, we sow seeds constantly. Perhaps it's money in the bank or a friendship you've cultivated over the years. Here and there we've invested time.

Almost everyone has someone they can call at three in the morning to pour their heart out to. Or a friend whose place they can stay at when the going gets tough.

Whatever you've been saving – emotionally, physically, financially – now is the time to use it. There is nothing more important in your life right now. This is the moment to cash in on everything you've worked for: every favor, every aspect of your friendships. The future has arrived and now is the time to harvest everything that you've worked for.

Take one step forward, and you're one step ahead of where you were.

HOW TO DRIVE THIS BOOK

Men aren't really good at giving relationship advice to other men. When we get ditched, our friends see it to it that we reach two important goals. The first is to get you drunk. The second is to get you some companionship. After those two stages have been completed, you are cured from whatever problems that have befallen.

In reality, there's slightly more to the healing process than those ancient gems of wisdom, passed down through the ages.

Men are logical creatures, almost to a fault. Emotional issues can be confusing and overwhelming to us, which is why a divorce is a painful event. What I am going to do is deconstruct the divorce and show you ways that I got through the pain by using logic.

Men like analogies. Comparisons help us formulate a picture in our head better than any other teaching method.

Men like analogies.

In this book, there is overlap. My ideas and observations aren't as clear-cut as building something – inserting Tab A into Slot B. Parts of what I talk about layer on top of one another, or dovetail nicely with each other.

It's like making a lasagna; the noodles, cheese and sauce meld into each other. Once it gets baked, there isn't any clear division between the different ingredients. And there you have it, the first analogy of the book.

The other way that guys deal with their issues is by diving into them. When we build something, we gather the materials, tools and manuals (which we seldom read) - then we get busy.

You have within you the materials to get through this process: Friends, family, a sense of self-worth, and the desire to move on with your life. The manual hasn't been written, that's what you're going to do.

This book, although it may appear like a "How To" manual, is more about providing you with tools than an exact process. How you apply them is up to you. Results may vary from person to person. These tools may also be utilized in other parts of your life, once you've gotten yourself back on track.

My pain and suffering was just as real as yours is right now. I found a way out of this mess, by moving forward. Within you, is the ability to heal yourself and create a new and exciting life for yourself.

Excerpts from the journal I kept during my divorce appear in *italics*.

Without any more hype, let's get down to it. The only way through this is by diving into the belly of the beast. As William Shakespeare said in Henry V, "Once more unto the breach, dear friends."

SURVIVAL TECHNIQUE

Are you scared, angry and hurt? Good, that means you're alive! While some of my statements might seem trite, even callous, there is nothing about this situation that I take lightly.

Some things may seem impossible. Everything and anything is possible.

Another way to look at this journey is like a mountain climb. If you try to visually take in the entire peak – with its jagged precipices, raging rivers and snow-capped peak - it seems impossible. So, you break it down. Start with getting your gear together, study the maps, then put one foot in front of the other. Examine the mountain in small quantities. Sure, you can look at the peak, but don't stress about it.

Break it down.

Concentrate on the next bend in the trail, the upcoming ledge that you'll need to cross. By tackling these elements in smaller, manageable units, you'll find that the summit isn't out of reach.

In and of themselves, the ledges and river-crossings might seem impassable. Concentrate on the task at hand and you'll find that you can get through. In the end, you won't die. Keep that mantra in the back of your head.

Where do we begin? First of all, accept that the marriage is over. Your wife is leaving you. In some ways, that is the hardest part of your journey. There is nothing that I can say or do to help you through this part. It's a leap of faith, an emotional detachment that you alone have to make. There is no way anyone can guide anyone else to that realization. Until you accept that, there is no sense going on with the rest of this book. After you admit to yourself that divorce is inevitable, you can move on.

Feel the pain, the unease, the uncertainty. Once you do, you can begin.

No, it's not going to be easy at first.

LOGISTICS

You might find yourself in the awkward situation of having to divide your items and one of you will have to move out. My suggestion is that you be the one to relocate. Staying in the old house or apartment will only force you to live among the ghosts.

It's amazing how anything from a certain pillow, a favorite picture on the wall or even the way you prepare food in the kitchen can set you off. Start anew. If possible, get your own place or move in with a friend. But I don't recommend staying in the same place that you lived with your wife. Be the nice guy and let her stay and inherit the past.

Moving allows you to clear out the deadwood in your life such as books, clothes and furniture. Now is the time to make a clean start. Out with the old, because this is your moment to begin a new life.

Easier said than done? Absolutely. This will be a massive task. I was in an emotional place where I didn't know what I wanted to do. Stay in my current city or move? Find a new line of work or stick with what I know? Everything was in a flux.

If you feel like you don't know where to begin, that's OK. Nobody does.

Moving allows you to clear out the deadwood in your life.

My ex-wife and I tried therapy. When that didn't work and I realized that our marriage was finished, I felt helpless. With nowhere else to turn, I went to a final one-on-one session to get some perspective on where I was and what needed to be done. After that, I knew that I'd make better progress on my own - if I could get a plan together.

Even though my mind was whirling, I knew I had to make a completely fresh start. The pull of the past, the sentimentality, can be a dangerous anchor that won't allow you to move forward. Now is the time to break the chains and learn how to live your new life on your own terms.

TAKING CARE OF THE BODY

Let's take care of some basics. Despite the fact that you feel like you've been hit by a train and left in a heap by the roadside, only to be cited for littering; that's no reason to let your body go to shambles.

You've got to focus on taking care of one very important thing, despite all the pain you're going through. Respect your body. Your mind is a pile of radioactive goop right now, so save the physical part of yourself before it's too late!

Save the physical part of yourself before it's too late!

First of all, make sure you're getting enough sleep. If you're breaking down and crying like a blubbering baby, then you'll find sleep will come very easy. I was a regular snot-making machine, weeping until I felt like throwing up. Those gut wrenching sobs will do wonders for those of you reaching for the six-pack abs.

I can honestly say that I haven't slept as soundly before or after that era. No, I'm not wishing to go back to that time, just making a point.

Second, are you eating right? I found that I went from cooking for two people to just me. So, I stopped cooking and ate a lot of frozen foods. Eventually, I wasn't eating enough because I was depressed.

But when I did chow down, I went for the comfort food – high fat, high carbs, low on vitamins and other stuff you need. Now, I know that you feel like I'm burdening you.

If you fall into the fast food trap, you're going to feel worse. Your body is going through enough trouble - a radical change in your diet isn't going to help you. Chances are, you'll probably be eating out a lot more, so do it right.

Stay away from the greasy foods. Try some rice bowls or fresh salads. Just don't eat too many burgers and fries, they'll bog you down.

The last suggestion is going to cause you to throw this book down in a rage and pout on the couch, so get it out of your system now. You need to exercise.

I'm not saying you have to become a gym rat, but at least go for a walk, do some sit-ups or push-ups. Now, for those of you who just aren't into that, you're probably wondering, "I've never exercised before, so why should I start now?" Well, it helps you burn off anxious energy. It's also just plain healthy. I started biking twice as much as I did pre-divorce. It helped me slim down and it cleared my mind.

If you are unwilling or mentally incapable of doing any of these, then you're really making it more difficult to transition to your healing process. Also, by really focusing on making sure your body is doing well, you are nurturing and caring for yourself. This reinforces your independence.

Accept the fact that you came into this world alone and you're going to leave this world alone. That tells me that we were designed to function in this world alone.

It may not be fun, but it can be done. So prove to yourself that you are a self-sufficient human being.

It may be difficult and you may not feel like doing it. But I found that setting these attainable goals gave me a direction that would produce immediate benefits.

ROAD MAP

I am a map junkie. I used to work in a civil engineer's office to make money for college. I drew maps by hand before CAD-CAM came along and put guys like me out of work.

Ever since then, I've loved maps. I have boxes of them. Stacks of almanacs fill my book shelves. I guess the reason I'm infatuated with them is that no matter where you go in the world, they show you the way home.

Like every red-blooded male, I have to get the groundwork done before embarking on a journey.

For me, a day of running errands is better planned than a tactical military insertion. I know where I'm going, when and why.

Instead of crisscrossing the city, I plan my trip so I have all the right turns.

Why would I do any shopping before I go to the bank to deposit checks and get cash? That new pair of Nike shoes I need to buy can sit in the car. But I can't let the ice cream melt, which is why the grocery store is last.

Yes, you know exactly what I'm talking about. Planning is what makes men unique - because a well executed plan gives us more time to loaf around.

Efficiency breeds leisure.

So let's set up the road map of how you're going to get through this dark and mysterious forest.

Before I can launch into some unique examples of how I coped with my situation and the methods of dealing with divorce, I need to introduce you to a new mind-set.

Efficiency breeds leisure.

A lot of what I have to explain are logical examples based around a thought process that I believe most men possess. If you have a highlighter in one hand and package of Post-it notes near you, then I've proven my point.

However, the only way that that I can explain them is by tinkering with the traditional way we manage data based on methods that we acquire in life.

I'm asking for permission to re-wire how your thoughts are processed. Don't worry, it's not necessarily permanent.

If you don't like what I'm saying, just hit your reset button and go back to your usual process.

There might be times when you wonder – where is he going with all this?

Trust that I will connect everything after you understand a few simple concepts that I created to get me through to the other side. As we get further into the book, I will illustrate my methods that help to express a new definition of time, through examples.

I found that a lot of my issues with overcoming the divorce were due to my misguided perceptions. My old mode of understanding time locked me forever in the past, and prevented me from moving forward.

It took me months to understand how this old mechanism worked and how it imprisoned me. But after I accepted the new model, I was able to see the prison bars all around me. I merely needed to open the door and walk out. That's when things began to get clearer and I was able to start healing.

Keep in mind that when it comes time to rebuild your life – your empire – you need to build it out of stone. It takes a lot longer to work with rock, but you will have a solid fortress to protect and nurture you. Since now is the time to rebuild, do it right.

Also, how we communicate our feelings can fall short because of the limitations of language. Love is an example of the inadequacies of verbal interactions.

We love children and spouses, but we also love pizza, movies and fireworks. Love - is it overused, or is it an insufficient word to encapsulate how we feel?

Language cannot meet all the demands that the emotions require. But it's the best thing we have for right now.

Human time perception is based on our mastery of our native language. We have the **Past, Present and Future**, the three simple building blocks of time. Everything we have done, are doing and will do fit onto one of these blocks. But, these same blocks prevent us from fully experiencing what life has to offer. In essence, they prevent us from achieving greatness because of the rigid structure.

I'm going to smash the mold.

Keep in mind that sometimes I talk about a subject matter, then move in a new direction.

This is my way of planting seeds. Consider it a sneak peek of what will be coming up. This process of moving through a painful experience isn't necessarily a straight track, but a flowing river that changes course. Poetic, ain't it?

While some ideas may be repeated, they will be more fully developed concepts that relate to other ideas that I cover at different points throughout the book. What may seem to the untrained eye to be scattered thinking is really a well thought out book for two reasons.

First - by the end of this book, all the issues I discuss will dovetail into one, cohesive thought process that will hopefully help you cope with what you are going through.

The second reason is – well, I don't have one. This was my first divorce, so I'm new at all this deep suffering. All I can offer is that I was committed to getting out of my mess as efficiently as possible.

Before I talk more about the Past, Present or Future, I'll give you some background into my predicament.

STATISTICS

"A marital history was collected from each person in the household aged 15 and over. There were 69,571 people in the sample, from approximately 37,000 households."

Kreider, Rose M. and Jason M. Fields, 2001, *Number, Timing, and Duration of Marriages and Divorces Fall 1996*; Current Population Reports, P70-80; US Census Bureau Issued February 2002; p. 2.

In that study, "50 percent of first marriages for men under age 45 may end in divorce, and between 44 and 52 percent of women's first marriages may end in divorce for these age groups. The likelihood of a divorce is lowest for men and women age 60, for whom 36 percent of men and 32 percent of women may divorce from their first marriage by the end of their lives."

Ibid; p. 18

"Many people divorce, but the majority remarry. Most men and women may remarry after divorcing from a first marriage."

Ibid; p. 19

2

STATUS

MY JOURNEY

When I was forced to cope with the divorce, I had to deal with some difficult choices. What was most important to me was deciding where to live – remain in Los Angeles, retreat to Arizona where I lived for almost ten years, or even move back east to be near my family. The divorce was playing havoc with my sense of security.

My core beliefs were shaken, which affected my sense of identity. While I always considered myself confident and resilient, I had also looked at myself through the lens of a married man – not as an individual.

A few months before everything in my marriage broke loose, my ex-wife and I had spent Thanksgiving with my family. We shared a quiet Christmas day together, and spent that evening with the family of one of our friends. Even with the benefit of hindsight, I still cannot find any indication that anything was wrong with our marriage.

By the end of January, I was being hit with the fact that not all was well with our relationship. We attended a joint counseling session before I went away for a weekend. I felt that we needed to spend some time away from each other.

I had looked at myself through the lens of a married man - not as an individual.

We went to another joint session upon my return. It was then that the bomb was dropped. She wanted a divorce.

There was no room for negotiation, nothing that could be fixed or worked on. It was completely over between us. I realize now that she needed the safety and support of that session to make this announcement.

I left the session feeling completely numb. I literally couldn't feel hot or cold; it was like a bad dream. But I knew all too well that I wouldn't be waking up from this nightmare to a normal, happy marriage.

FEBRUARY 21

At our joint session, the therapist tells us that by the time you get to counseling, it's already too late for most people. I still held out for hope. Wrong that wasn't the smartest thing to do, it was already over in her eyes. I just hadn't gotten it yet. Previously, each of us met with the therapist alone - just to get to know him for a one on one session. Then we went to another joint session about a week later.

When I realized it was over – there was nothing left to work on. The Final Finality, as I later referred to it. The two of us walked to the car, and something inside me snapped. I really didn't remember walking down the stairs. I opened the car door - the ex had driven - then slammed it and ran. I mean RAN. I cruised, in dock-siders which aren't the best shoes in the world for that. I heard her yelling for me.

Like a cat with something on its tail - I boogied until I couldn't run anymore. I walked to a friend's house about four miles away. It felt good to work out all that nervous energy - he gave me a lift home that night. My ex had slept at a friend's house that night, obviously freaked out about this turn of events. I didn't have keys since she drove, so I had to break into my own house and sleep alone. I was overwhelmed. I had no emotional response to what was happening, it was too big to take in.

During my final one-on-one session, the therapist asked me about what happened that night. I guess my ex went back to the office concerned about my well being. Well, I had talked to my brother and a close friend on the phone after my hasty escape.

I assured them I just needed to be alone, but I wasn't going to do anything stupid. I mean, I can be emotional, but honestly, the thought of taking my life or hurting myself is just stupid. I've never gotten into a fight over a woman - please, if you want her bad enough, take her. Hurt myself over that, nope!

Why'd I run? It was all I could do, it was the only thing I had control over, my motion. I couldn't force the marriage to stay together, or force her to love me.

The only action that would obey my will was my movement. If I wanted to walk or run, that was up to me. So move I did! And man, if I wasn't leaving a scorched path behind me.

Right now, I'm clueless as to what the future holds. I don't know where to turn or what to do.

STUMBLING IN CIRCLES

It was a long, lonely journey, walking to my friend's house. The air was very damp and the streets were strangely empty. It's a bizarre feeling, wandering the streets, trying to get your mind around the fact that your life is about to change forever. It felt like I was about to undertake a monumental journey. One that ultimately ended up being happy, sad and incredibly life changing. This isn't to say that I was looking forward to it.

But when change stares you down, you can either control it or let it control you. I had no intention of passively going along for the ride. Now was the time for action, but what was I supposed to do?

I had no idea how I was going to go about this. Marriage doesn't come with a manual or a warranty card. I spent countless hours in book stores looking for information on how to deal with what I was going through.

Change: control it, or let it control you.

The material dealt with divorce from the women's point of view, from the family perspective, or from a clinical stance.

But there was nothing that could help me get through my struggle from the male perspective – rational, precise, and with a clear-cut goal.

Sometimes being too logical tends to suppress the emotional component. There is an equilibrium to be met between the two. Eventually, I was able to perform the difficult balancing act so that I could break through my pain and find inner peace.

After starting to deal with my pain, I decided to visit the therapist one more time for a solo session.

MARCH 1

I found out that she wanted to go to therapy to get clarity on the situation and find out a way to preserve the friendship. It wasn't really about saving the marriage.

I'm not against friendship down the road - though I don't feel like it right now, I will concede. See, the vibe right now is - I'm trying to get through a DIVORCE here, can we deal with this other angle later – the feeling about being friends will wait, 'cause I'm just not there yet!

OK, I spent about two weeks of my life trying to work and keep busy - in between crying my eyes out. Tell you one thing, cry yourself exhausted and you'll sleep great. Works for babies. I tell people, you have trouble sleeping, do something to make yourself cry - like the sissy boy you are. I'm talking icicles of snot, dripping from your nose to the floor, your eyes a river of tears, your stomach tired of contracting from all the sobs welling up from your bowels. Yeah, sounds grim, and it is for sure. I don't want to do that again. But at least I sleep great every night!

For now, I'm past the crying part - see, if someone doesn't want to be with you for ANY reason - well, what can you do about it? I mean, you're simply cast free, either fight it tooth and nail (most likely really setting off the other person) or be adult about it. Things change, don't take it personally, that's what the therapist said. Good advice.

Sounds great on paper, it's another thing to put it into practice. But reality is - keep your eye on that goal, and you'll get there. I'm not there yet, but hey, it's a process. Right now, I'm packing stuff up.

MARCH 3

So, I told my therapist that I didn't know what to do with my life next, do I want to stay in LA or move? More questions than answers, and I didn't know where to begin.

How about some travel, he said. Aw, com'on, I haven't got time for that, I gotta find a place, 'cause I got nowhere to go, and.....

-- then it hit me, the proverbial light-bulb over the head. The sky parted, angels flitted down from heaven, as a shaft of light illuminated my body. And then thought came to me: I was hungry and could really go for a burrito.

Well, that was my second or third thought. No, the primary thought was - sure, travel as in WHOOSH!

GAMEPLAN

The therapist and I discussed my plans for the future. Or rather, he broached the subject and I talked. It was brief, as I had no plans. My whole life was tied into goals set with my wife. My therapist knew I had traveled extensively on solo trips as well as vacations with my wife.

He suggested I go on a trip as a way to get myself back together again. I immediately discounted this. There were work obligations. I needed to find a place to live. Surely, this was not the time for a vacation.

However, he wasn't suggesting a vacation, but a trip that would give me time to think. The more I pondered it, the more I realized that taking time off for a trip would be a physical manifestation of my inner journey.

Slowly, images formed in my head over the next few days. I felt that I needed to remove myself from anything familiar, eradicate any crutch and dive right into myself. Staying in Los Angeles wasn't an option, not if I wanted to remain there. Strange as it sounds, I needed to leave if I ever wanted to consider staying.

I needed to leave if I ever wanted to consider staying.

Leaving would allow me to look at the structure of my life from the outside. At that instant in my life, there were too many regrets, too much pain. I needed something new, something that was mine. Staying in Los Angeles would've caused me to depend too much on my friends.

I was also starting to get into a rut with the same depressing story that was slowly turning into a mantra. It was time to scratch the record, destroy that destructive cycle and begin anew.

I was able to wrap up the work projects I was involved in. Then I began packing up everything that was mine: books, photos, clothes.

Even though I was angry and hurt by my wife's decision, I knew it would physically be easier for me to move. I was able to lug the boxes to storage in the back of my truck, whereas she would've needed some help. Also, I didn't want to stay in a home that we picked out together. Without her there, I knew that the memories would haunt me.

Moving also gave me an opportunity to clear out the deadwood and streamline my life.

How does one begin to cope with the reality of divorce? Where do you start? Let's begin with a concept of what marriage is. I'm not talking about in terms of the vows you exchanged or some religious angle.

It's time to:

UNDERSTAND THE ENTITIES

In a marriage, there are really three, that's right, **three** entities: You, Her and the Marriage.

Marriage can be a blissful coexistence between two people when there is a unification of two souls melding together into one unit.

The marriage in and of itself is a separate entity. While I'm not trying to promote any religion here, the Bible does have a passage in Genesis 2:24 that says:

"For this reason a man will leave his father and mother and be united to his wife, and the two will be one flesh."

First of all, it tells me that the two will be having sex, uniting together to create "one flesh".

More importantly, the passage illustrates that a new, third entity is created. This "one flesh" is the entity of marriage.

Unfortunately, during a divorce, you are losing two thirds of what you once had. You lose the marriage, and your wife. If you're not careful, then you may lose yourself and be left with nothing. That's the purpose of this book, to save the remaining 33%.

This is why divorce is so tragic, because more is lost than you had realized.

During a divorce, you are losing two thirds of what you once had.

So, how do you deal with losing 66% of an identity? Nurture yourself. It's an easy concept - two simple words. I understand they are very difficult to digest and live. But what choice do you really have? You are in a mental and spiritual life and death situation. This is you call to arms.

Right now, your focus should be about creating or re-creating a strong sense of the self. Granted, it might seem as if everything is gone. But you are living and breathing. Take stock in that.

Here's another concept that will be discussed in greater detail later. I mention it here so you can put it into the back of your mind to see what gels.

During this period, you will be mining seemingly small and insignificant strengths that will allow you to discover your inner strength. Take this in.

Don't skip ahead, just stay with me.

MOVING OUT

OK, I was able to move my stuff out of the house. It was the most difficult thing I've ever done, physically and emotionally. I accomplished this by focusing on what had to get done in the moment.

Let that sink in: *Focus on what absolutely has to happen now!*

I want that to mull around in the back of your head along with the three entities, which are:

OK recap. You, Your wife, Your marriage.

Oh, I can hear you clamoring now. You want to skip to the "good stuff" like you did when you set up your home entertainment system.

Focus on what absolutely has to happen now.

Don't do it. This book isn't that long, and I need to introduce another concept before we really dive into it. No short cuts.

Moving out has many different paths radiating from it. There is personal property that needs to be divided, and possibly real estate, such as a house. Bank accounts need to be severed, utilities might be in both of your names, so that needs to be handled. Health and auto insurance, joint car loans, the list goes on and on.

Don't get overwhelmed. If you need to hire a lawyer or speak with an accountant, then do it.

The point is, try to focus on what you can change right now. That sounds like an oversimplification of what you have to deal with. But that is one goal you have to aim for.

We'll go through some more concepts before we circle back to this point.

LET IT OUT

Before we go too much further into my thought processes, I need to discuss something you could very well be going through now. I've touched on it already, but time to face the truth.

You've probably been crying or on the verge of tears. Yeah, real men don't cry. Sure, tell yourself that. I hadn't cried in years before this mess.

It's not that I consciously suppressed emotional scars - I just had nothing to cry about.

During this crisis, I had plenty to cry about. While on that topic, I want to emphasize that a crisis isn't necessarily a negative occurrence. A crisis is a crucial event or turning point. Some are more dangerous than others.

But no matter how much they threaten us, we are presented with a choice.

Choice is something I am going to be constantly reminding you about. No matter what happens, each individual is responsible for his own reaction or emotional feelings towards an event.

For now, I want emphasize that it's OK to let your guard down, feel vulnerable and human and cry. While I'm not advocating that you need to let it all out at work or in front of your friends 24/7, you do need to give yourself permission to let yourself feel the pain and cry.

EMOTIONAL MELTDOWNS

Throughout the whole process, you are bound to have Emotional Meltdowns. This can range from having a bad day to an all out mental collapse, and every shade in between.

However, these meltdowns need to be embraced and even fanned to really get the flames going. No, this is not insanity, but a way to purge them out of your body.

Look at your emotional core as a forest. Instead of having healthy trees and fields of grass that stretch to the horizon, you now have withered branches and brown grass dotting the landscape. In order to begin anew, you must burn it all down.

Controlled burns are what the forestry service does to remove diseased trees or overgrown forests.

Well, they do now, instead of following their ancient and narrow-minded zero-tolerance policy for fires that allowed the forests to collect too much deadwood and undergrowth.

As a result, forest fires reached apocalyptic proportions, leaving the land looking like a war zone. That's what happens when you don't clean house.

But I digress. The burn gets rid of all the dead wood, and the ashes create a nutrient layer that fosters new growth. Pine cones need the heat to burst open, so the seeds can be released.

In the legend of the Phoenix, the aging bird builds a nest of wood that is set on fire. From its ashes, a new bird emerges. It is this emotional rebirth that should be yet another one of your goals.

The downside is that it can be very difficult process. But if the flames of the Emotional Meltdown are constantly squashed, then your pains cannot be purged.

A part of you – most likely a very large part – is trying to hold on to the past.

3

STRATEGY

MEMORY ELEMENTS

Memory Elements are the defining moments in your relationship, such as a favorite song, a special restaurant or an anniversary.

When you hear a favorite song, it projects negative emotions such as loneliness, sorrow and sadness. Whatever reaction you feel about that song isn't because of the memory element, but because of the negative haze around it.

Men need examples, I know I do.

Imagine a damp, cloudy day near the beach. Everything seems dreary, the colors are washed out. This might seem like a bad day.

Then the sun comes out, and the cloud cover burns off. The temperature rises, and the colors of the trees, houses and sand burst to life. This turns into a good day.

The day is still the same, the colors of the houses were always there, but the cloud cover had changed your *perception* of it.

Your memory elements, the cherished memories, aren't bad. You need to remove your **Emotional Filter**, because it is distorting your view of how things really were.

DIAGRAM 1

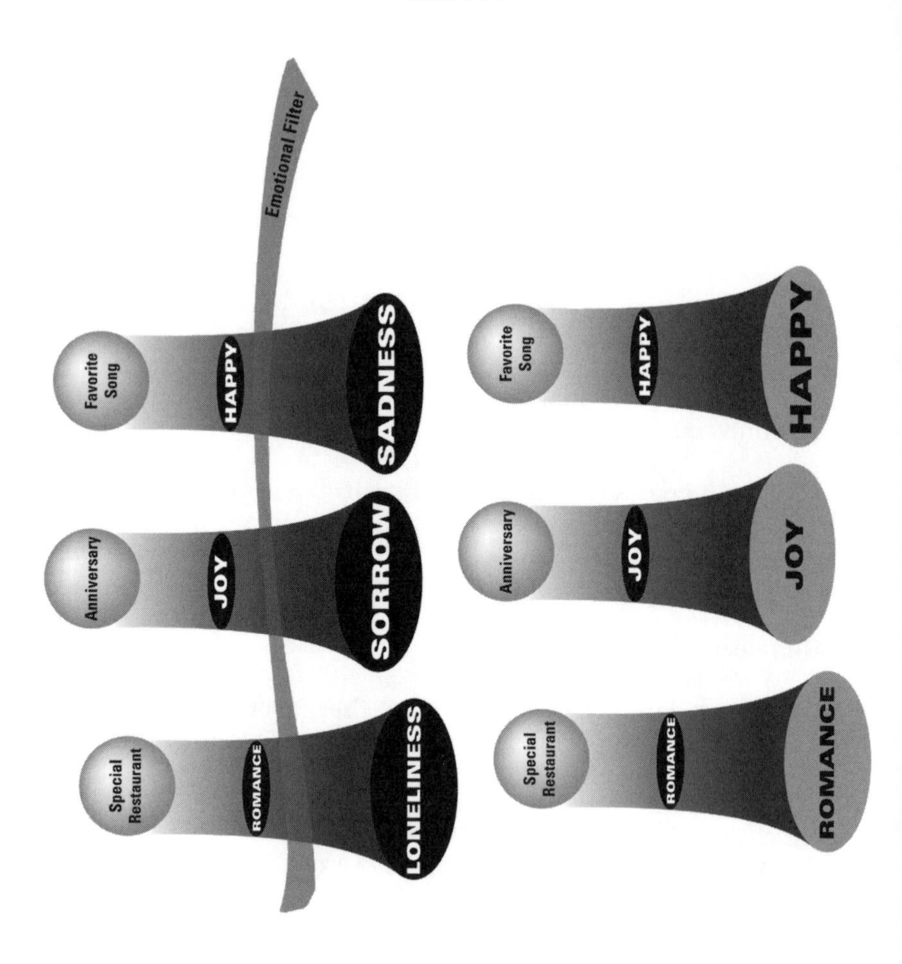
Emotional Filter
Favorite Song
HAPPY
SADNESS
Anniversary
JOY
SORROW
Special Restaurant
ROMANCE
LONELINESS
Favorite Song
HAPPY
HAPPY
Anniversary
JOY
JOY
Special Restaurant
ROMANCE
ROMANCE

CONFRONT THE MEMORIES

You're probably thinking - How? I'm in a lot of pain, so I can't reflect on these memories without hurting more!

Recognize that the memory elements are not going to change. They are facts. You **did** celebrate your anniversaries together, you did share a favorite song.

As I said already, your *perception* of these elements causes you pain. The negative, emotional filter isn't giving you a clear view of how things are.

If you try to focus on getting your emotions under control, you won't succeed.

I want you to work smart, not hard.

What we are doing is actually **saving** the memories.

PULL THE FILTER

Removing the filter doesn't give the whole story. If it were only that easy! It's more like pulling out a splinter.

The next time you hear that favorite song or think about that special restaurant, allow yourself to feel the pain. Give yourself the right to say, "We'll never have breakfast there together again" or "We'll never hug each other on the sofa while listening to that song."

What does it feel like? For me, it was like my guts were being ripped out of my body, while I was getting kicked. Then I felt like I was tossed off a cliff and into a cactus garden. And those were my good days.

Most of the time, I ended up crying harder than I ever had before in my life. Your results may differ.

The natural reaction to all your pain is to pack that memory away. You try to convince yourself that by not thinking about it, you'll somehow save it from getting damaged.

Fear not, your memories are incredibly resilient. By hiding from your past recollections, you are hoping that things will work out between the two of you. Denying that the relationship is over is not the place to go. It may seem like the easy route, but don't take it. It will only thrust you deeper into the hole.

While you are going through this new process your mind and body are finding a new way to cope with these memory elements. Your mind is trying to shut down from the emotional overload by frantically hitting the "Escape" key. Don't let your mind shy away from this pain. The status quo has been shattered; you need to deal with it.

The good news is, while you are crying through your pain, you're not going to die.

But, the bad news is, while you are crying through your pain - you're not going to die - though you might wish you had.

BUCK UP LITTLE CAMPER!

Now doesn't that phrase just fill you with contempt? It isn't an uplifting tag line, but a patronizing, smug statement. When people tell you to do that, keep smiling, maintain eye contact, and step away. Let the anger subside. Realize that the best intentions can sometimes produce negative results.

It's OK to ask people to stop trying to help you.

Back to the crying issue. Your body will get tired of weeping, the heaving sobs will end and you'll probably be physically wiped out. Soon, you'll feel an overwhelming desire to sleep. Go for it - you've earned it.

What can't be put into words, because it's different for everyone, is that your emotional filter is being pulled out very slowly. Eventually, your mind will give up associating pain with all the memory elements, simply because it'll get too tired to fight. While you're surveying your memories, allow yourself to have emotional meltdowns.

They can come in all shapes and sizes. You might be at the grocery store buying oatmeal, only to realize that you hate the stuff but are used to buying it for your ex-wife. It could be a small moment - a spark, or it could be huge - we're talking nuclear.

Through this process, I would highly recommend staying away from photographs. If there are any photo albums, put out of sight for now. There's a difference between how you remember things in your mind versus how the reality appears when it's staring back at you in a photograph.

When you realize that you are able to look back on the memories that you created with your ex-wife, without any meltdowns, is the moment when your emotional filter is completely removed.

Stay away from photo albums.

ACTIONS AND BELIEFS

I reached this thought process because I realized a long time ago that humans have a great deal of conflict between their **actions** and their **beliefs**. When I first started driving, I felt guilty about speeding. I was young and idealistic, and if someone really believes that all laws should be obeyed, then nobody should ever speed on the highways.

However, I'd feel like it was taking forever to get around, so I'd increase up my speed a little bit. After all, I knew the highways so well I could drive them in my sleep. We all have many different rationales: "The other people on the highway were going faster than I was." or "The highway was empty. Who am I going to hurt?" or "I was only going 5 miles an hour over the speed limit." Eventually, I was able to exceed the speed limits and not feel guilty about it.

How? Simple. I stopped believing that what I was doing was morally wrong. Obviously, I couldn't state that I believed it was illegal, because my actions proved otherwise. This may sound like rationalization - it isn't.

Rationalization starts when people proclaim that they believe in something specific. When they don't live up to that belief, they give an explanation as to why they don't live by the same rules that they expect others to obey.

An example of this is someone who declare that we have to save the environment by driving efficient vehicles. Then they climb into their albatrosses that get five gallons to the mile. They rationalize it by saying they like the safety of a big vehicle or a smaller vehicle won't fit all their groceries.

If they simply said that they think everyone should have the right to drive a land yacht, they can't be accused of not following their own beliefs.

What I am suggesting is the sometimes it's easier to change your beliefs than it is your actions.

I had a friend who thoroughly enjoyed chocolate. Almost every time she ate it, she felt guilty afterwards. There were too many calories...it isn't good for the body...too much sugar. I finally suggested that she stop believing that chocolate was bad for her, since she didn't show any signs of stopping. Once she did, the guilt was gone.

TIME IN THREE TENSES

Time is that elusive ingredient that surrounds us everyday, yet we don't know how to manage it, nor can we accurately define it. You can't taste it or see it, yet we can never run away from it. Time is always there.

I am going to spell out my concept of time. You really need to understand my concept, because everything else that I discuss is based on this platform.

This is coming from a guy who flunked college calculus because I didn't take the time to study the fundamentals. Don't gloss over this. I'm not going to delve into quantum mechanics or Einstein's theory of relativity, mostly because I'm not sure what either one of them are.

THE PAST

What happened yesterday, or years before, is behind us, in the conventional method of thinking. The fact that your marriage is over is now in the past. It happened before you even picked up this book. But is it really in the past?

Not at all, because it is affecting how you think and feel in this moment. Your interactions with other people will be forever altered because of this past knowledge. You might shut down, become angry or resentful because of your reaction to past events.

It's important to realize that the actions of the past are with us everyday. We learn our present lessons because of our past reactions.

Bobby Gallant gets yelled at by Johnny Rude on the school playground. Gallant now feels hurt by the incident. He may become reclusive, avoid that person, or even fight back. His response is, it's in relation to a past event.

Gallant might tell his parents, "Johnny Rude said something mean to me at school this morning."

The facts – raw, unemotional, and honest – are all spoken about in the past tense. However, the emotional response that's generated shape Gallant in the present.

On an emotional level, there is no past, only the present.

The above is absolutely correct and cannot be disputed - and I'll find some important scientist to back it up with graphs and published papers if necessary. So don't argue with me and we'll keep going.

If Bobby Gallant were to see Johnny Rude at this very moment, Gallant's actions toward Rude would be based on past memories.

THE PRESENT

The present is the now - what's right in front of us. Sounds simple, but do people really live in the now? Do they feel, taste and accept what is happening to them in this very moment?

At first blush, it would seem that most people exist happily in the now. I am convinced that the majority of us live in the past. I know that I have.

Are you wallowing in yesterday, dredging up past abuses or perhaps living off the glory of a previous victory? While sifting through memories can be useful, fun and even enlightening, getting too melancholy about past events can prevent you from fully experiencing the now.

To truly be in the now is to feel the wind on your face without comparing it to anything in the past. I remember a friend of mine explaining to me that ancient masters of the martial arts would set a task before their students.

The eager youths had to walk from one side of the room to the other and only think of the act of walking from one wall to the other, before they could learn anything else. It took some students years to master that task.

Why would that task be so difficult? It's simple - the past intrudes on the mind. This creates an anxiety of the future, causing one to stumble through the present. People state that they want to live life to the fullest, live in the now. But how does this translate into what they really want?

Many times, it's about a big, upcoming trip, a new purchase of a material good, eating at a restaurant with friends. But does anyone actually say – I am enjoying the moment, right here, right now?

I've found myself wondering how much better dessert will be, even while I'm on the main course - never really looking around and just enjoying that exact moment in time.

When you truly enjoy the moment is when you don't look to the past for justification that, "Yes, everything is better today than it was yesterday." Rather, you are enjoying every second based on its merits.

THE FUTURE

In the spoken language, this element of time is something that hasn't happened yet. It's on the horizon. It could be in the next few minutes, or years away.

The problem with the future is that we are basing our perceptions of that possible period in time on what happened to us in the past.

For example, if I am thinking about an upcoming party with friends, I will be wondering – will a certain person be there that I like or dislike; how will the food be; will I find parking this time or have to drive around for hours looking for a space?

These are very trivial, basic examples. But upon reflection, it will become clear that a prediction, or an expectation, is being made.

This *invention* of the future in our mind is molded by past events. While all these thoughts are going on, the present is slipping by completely unnoticed and unappreciated because our mind is focusing on past and future.

We are trying to qualify the 'what may or may not happen' based on similar events that did or did not happen.

DIAGRAM 2

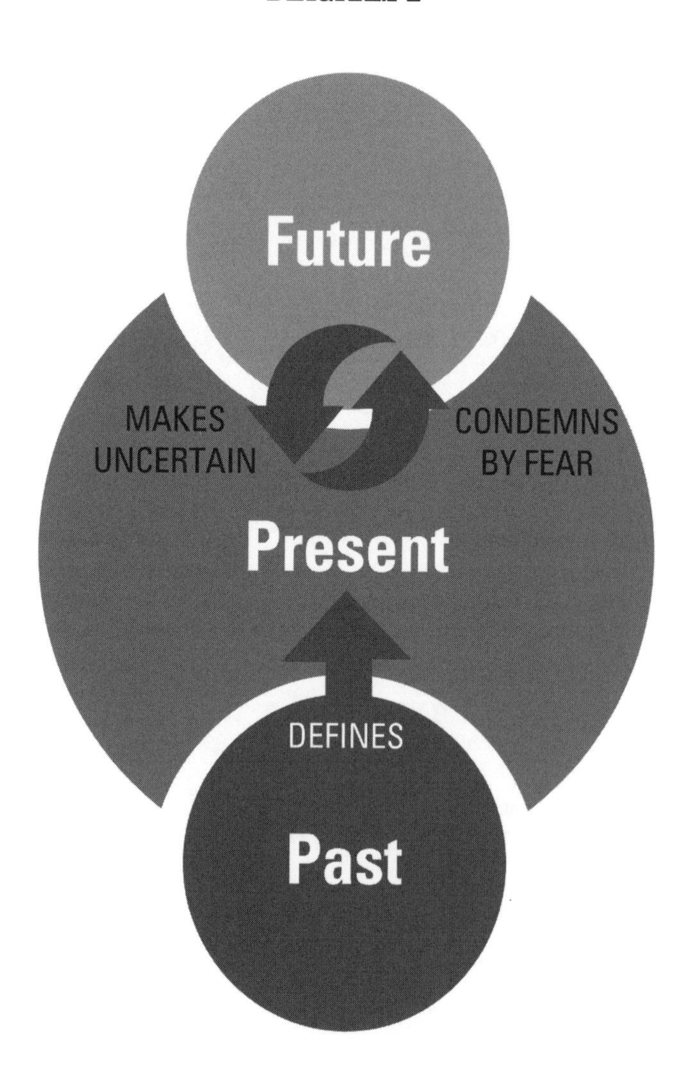
Future
MAKES UNCERTAIN
CONDEMNS BY FEAR
Present
DEFINES
Past

4

RECONNAISSANCE

SYNTHESIS

There is a way to fuse the past, present and future into one thought process.

Synthesis is a way to truly be in the present, while keeping an oblique eye on the past and future. It's a way of thinking that eliminates the pain of the past, and the restrictions of the future, by not having expected notions of either time frame.

This does not mean there is no more planning, ever. Think ahead about buying a home, going to school, taking a trip. But instead of making it the center of attention, it lies off the periphery. It's like something you catch out of the corner of your eye.

The idea is to keep the past and the future just a little foggy and on the edges of your focus.

MIND AND MANUAL FOCUS EXERCISE

What you are going to do is stare at a point on the wall. Just look at it. Keep focusing.

Put your hand up on either side of your face, about a foot away and just far enough off to the side that you can see it out of your peripheral vision. Keep your eyes focused on the point that you selected.

Without moving your eyes or your hands, I want you to:

Concentrate on your left hand.

Then focus on the point on the wall.

Now, focus on your right hand.

Finally, focus back on the point on the wall.

Your hands will be a bit fuzzy, but you'll get a new sensation as you focus on the hand.

Do this a few times, **without moving your eyes.** I want you to realize the **sensation** you're feeling while you do this.

Go ahead and try this technique now. When you're done, we'll continue.

MIND FOCUS

Was it a new sensation, being able to "look" at another object, without turning your head? Was it easier to focus back and forth as you practiced?

I call this **Mind Focus**.

Now, try the same exercise, except this time, **move your eyes** back and forth between the point on the wall and either hand. Perform this exercise a few times.

MANUAL FOCUS

What did you notice that was different from not moving your eyes? It probably took you a little longer to concentrate on each object, simply because your eyes had to focus their lens between your hands and the point on the wall.

This second type of focus, I call **Manual Focus**.

Restore you hands to where they were before.

FINAL EXERCISE

Do these exercises again – in both the **Mind Focus** mode and the **Manual Focus** mode. Shift back and forth between the two methods. Again, focus on the **sensation** you get when you do each one of them; then we'll continue.

WRAP UP

You'll probably find that the Mind Focus allows the senses to rapidly shift back and forth between different objects.

How does all this tie into the perception of **Past, Present** and **Future**?

The left hand represents the **Past**; the point on the wall is the **Present**; the right hand is the **Future**. Instead of looking back and forth between the two hands by turning your head (Manual Focus), you may find that you are more efficient at going back and forth between past, present and future by not turning your eyes or head (Mind Focus).

If you want to play with this further, try holding up something with different colors to it and really focus on the colors, shape and texture by not moving your head.

DEFINITIONS

Mind Focus – You **don't** move your head because you're letting your **mind** do the focusing.

Manual Focus – You move your head or eyes so you are **manually** bringing the object into focus.

NEW THOUGHT PROCESS

Are you having fun? Is this something new for you? Are you wondering where this is all going? Well, let's keep moving forward then. This is your journey.

The first step to creating a new thought process is to be able to shift your focus by using the Mind Focus. Most of the time, your attention should be on the present, with past and present in the periphery.

Think of the future as a nefarious cloud - nothing is set, and it can change at any time.

These things on the outskirts of your vision could be a party with friends, buying a house, or a new job. Keep them just out of your center focus, but within your presence.

There will be a time and place to make these elements in the future become objects of great importance – it is at that time we are able to perform a Manual Focus, and really delve into that subject matter. When the time comes to buy that house, you will turn your head and eyes onto that issue. It will then be the center of your purpose, and everything else will fall into the periphery.

Let's use a simple example – buying a car. If you focus on buying a car and you don't have the money to buy one, or just really don't need one, or are too lazy to shop for one, then stop thinking about it. Don't waste time with a Manual Focus on that subject matter. It's clear that you don't have the means to follow through with it at that time. Push it back to the periphery, and continue with your focus and enjoyment of the present.

The real prize is when you can achieve **Synthesis**.

This is where you can focus on Past, Present and Future at the same time.

Neither has weight over the other; all three time frames hold the same water. A new, overall focus comes into play. We'll come back to Synthesis later.

The concepts of Manual Focus and Mind Focus will be utilized to examine some core issues that are going on at this time.

You're probably thinking that this is all easier said than done. It can be difficult, but not impossible.

We're going to put the Mind Focus and Manual Focus aside for now. There are some other concepts that we need to be clear on. You'll see that they'll converge rather quickly.

TOOLBOX

Your rebuilding process is like building furniture. You spend a lot of time measuring and cutting wood. You've got stacks of different pieces, some with rough edges. The next step will be to assemble and sand it. Once you start nailing components together, it starts to take shape. For now, we're still cutting lumber.

Are you having any thoughts such as, *I'll never be loved again* or, *I'll never get married again* and even, *My life as I know it, is over*? If so, shut them down, because these aren't issues that you can even address at this time. Let's continue and you'll see what I mean.

Negative thoughts flooded through my mind constantly. There's no doubt that it was overwhelming. In order to move on, the cycle had to be broken. I'm going to show you how to break the cycle.

You are most likely in a state of extreme hurt. The first thing you need to understand is that you are able to make a choice. Finding what choices are attainable can be found by realizing what you **don't** have a choice over.

FEWER CHOICES CAN MAKE IT EASIER

Will the marriage be fixed or is it definitely over? If there is absolutely no chance of reconciling, then smile. That's one decision you don't have to make. You no longer have control of it. That finality brought me great relief.

Right now, what you can choose is between being miserable, or being happy. This is really what it comes down to, when you reduce everything to its most basic level.

Even your quantity of happiness and misery lies solely in your hands. You can get through this and learn to be happy again, but you've got to take that one step in the direction.

This is probably one of the hardest choices to make, but once you choose to leave the misery behind, you'll see it's the only way to go.

My pain was so intense at times that going to the grocery store to get food was a chore. My work suffered because I couldn't concentrate on my job. Eventually, I decided to take charge and find away out of the pain.

BYE-BYE MISERY...FOR NOW

If you choose to wallow in misery, I can understand your hurt, pain and sorrow. If you actively choose not to be happy, then close this book. That's it, because there is no room for hope.

But if you can muster up the courage inside you to be happy, then you can get through this. This is an important step in the journey of a thousand miles.

OK, so I'm assuming that you decided to be happy, or you wouldn't be reading this right now. I'm going to take you through a simple exercise that can help you get through some of the rougher spots you may hit. Realize that some days are harder than others.

You are going to recognize how much pain you can accept, and make it manageable.

PAIN THRESHOLD

Now that we've talked about a perception of time, the next concept that needs to be understood is how much pain you can withstand. This requires brutal honesty with the self. You don't want to shy away from what could be a deep understanding of some of the core issues in your life. Look into the heart of the beast, and remember that you'll come out alive.

If you can manage this step, the breakthrough on the other side can be beautiful and life changing for the better.

Just believe, and push forward through the maze of trees, rocks and paths to nowhere. Move forward.

How do you actually manage the pain? As you examine your present situation, break it down into smaller units. For example, if you can't sit and really mull over some of the realities facing you for an hour at a time, break it down into four separate, 15-minute sessions of deep concentration per day. If that doesn't work, keep breaking it down until you reach a manageable level.

It's a lot like training for an extreme sport. A divorce can feel like a triathlon – where you run, swim and bicycle all in one day.

Break pain down into smaller units.

Unless you've been through a divorce before, you most likely don't have the emotional and mental skills to deal with it. Like jogging, you don't start by running twenty-six miles. You do a little each day, gradually building up to greater distances.

For me, I had a hard time deciding what I was going to do with my life. So, I started small. What you are going to accomplish will combine the concept of Mind Focus and Manual Focus with the Pain Threshold.

DIAGRAM 3

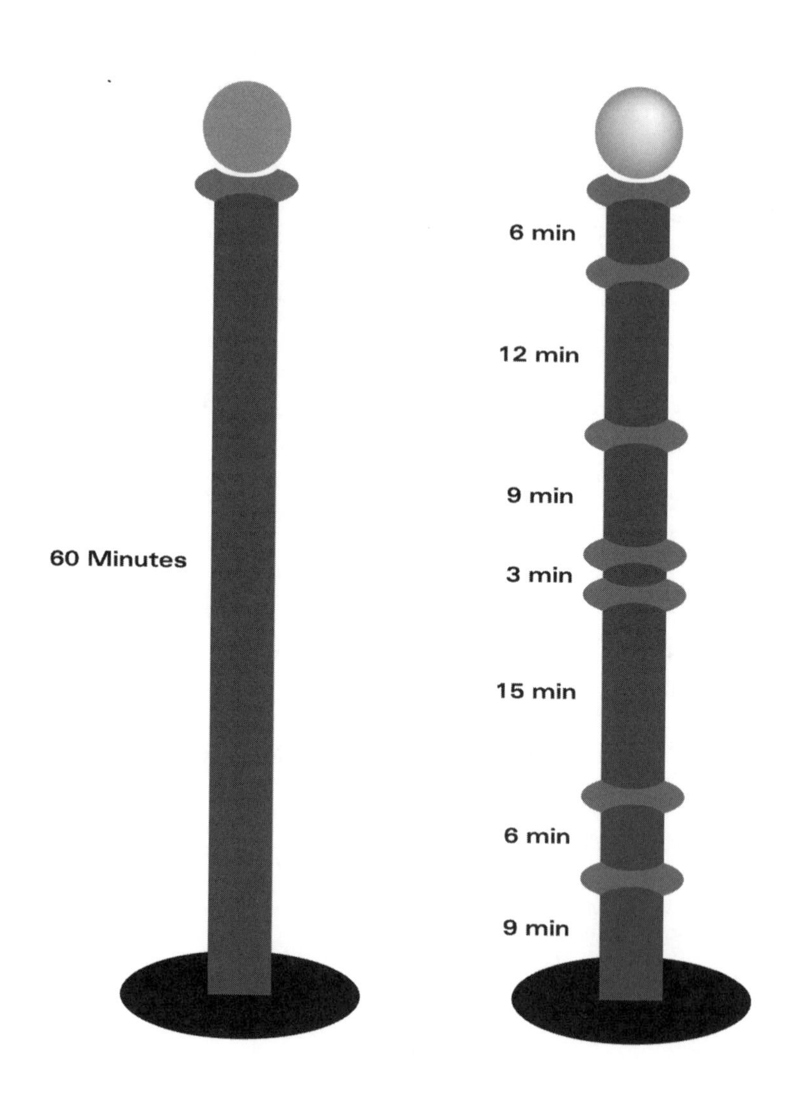

5

ORGANIZE

TIME TO MOVE

My wife and I decided that she was going to stay in the house we were renting and I would move out. At that moment in time, I knew I had to pack up my belongings.

But which ones were mine to take?

At this point, I was using Mind Focus to discover what it was I had to do. Deciding whether or not I would fall in love again, where I would live, what I would be doing a year from then, simply wasn't important.

If I never packed up my belongings, none of that would happen. Preparing to move was my first step in my journey of a thousand miles.

Some days, I took my Mind Focus and Manual Focus to the extreme. In order for me to decide what to pack up, I would have to get out of bed, shower, get dressed and eat before I could even decide what to pack.

Without addressing those basic needs, nothing else would happen in my life. If I didn't get out of bed, I couldn't eat, if I didn't eat, I wouldn't have energy to pack up the boxes. No boxes packed up, can't move nor can I get on with my life. Therefore, if I don't get my sorry butt out of bed, I'll never get on with my life.

When you find that you don't know what to do, start taking smaller steps. But never stop moving - always go forward.

WHEN PACKING UP YOUR CARES, DITCH THE WOES

It was time to pack some stuff. Books were easy since there wasn't too much literature we bought together as we had different tastes in our reading. I bought some boxes and packed up my books, labeled the boxes, then set them in a corner.

At this point, without even realizing it, I was making headway. I was focusing on something that had to happen in order for me to move on with my life. I also broke up what needed to be done into manageable units by recognizing my Pain Threshold.

These may sound like basic, almost childish routines to go through. But I needed to learn how to walk again before I could run.

My next step was to rent a storage unit to put all my belongings into. Why? I was still looking at the possibility of taking a trip out of the country. Even if I did back out and move into my own place, all my personal effects would be in one place. I made a plan and I stuck with it.

Day after day, more of my items got packed away. I would load up my truck and take them to my storage unit less than a mile away. Then, when the time came for us to divide up our communal items, I was on a roll and ready to deal with that. Letting go is something that will seem very natural in a short period of time.

For now, understand that by using the tools of Manual/Mind Focus and Pain Threshold, I was able to regain control of my life again. By finding tasks that needed to get done, I took my mind of my emotional pain.

However, I had other emotional issues that I needed to align in my life. I wasn't out of the woods yet. I wasn't even close.

MARCH 14

What is the dealio with divorce? According to my therapist 50% of all marriages end up in divorce, actually I think he said 54%. So statistically, anybody's marriage comes down to a coin toss. How 'bout that for a new wedding ceremony?

-- And now, the groom's family will toss the coin - the bride will call it in the air. You win the toss, the marriage will blossom, you lose - well, we'll roll a twenty sided die to see how long you two stick it out!

And you know what else he said - well you probably don't so I won't try to build up the suspense. Outta those remaining 50% of successful marriages, maybe 1 in 4 is really solid - and most of those are second marriages! So that means only 10% of all marriages are good ones.

Oh great, that's just reassuring. If 50% of all soft drinks made you sick, or 50% of all vehicles ended up in fatal accidents - the government would outlaw them in a second. But a 50% failure rate on marriage and the government isn't stopping us from doing something so risky. The odds ain't good, yet thousands of people do it every year. Stop the insanity!

Got an appointment with a lawyer next week. We already divided our stuff up, but we figured it just makes sense to have someone do all the legal paperwork, don't want to find out in three years that we were never divorced. My plan is to walk away from this whole thing come April 3, I mean if I never want to see her again, so be it. Not wishing her any evil or hard-ship. It's just that when this is done, it's done.

EMOTIONAL REACTION TO DIVORCE

Another issue I had with my divorce was that I viewed my past with disdain. I began to regret ever getting married. After all, since we were about to be divorced, what was the point of being married? I felt that I had wasted almost six years of my life with this woman. I had doomed the past to a dark recess of my mind.

How could we have chosen so poorly? What had I done to deserve such a fate? Why did I have to suffer through all this? Such thoughts create a downward spiral of despair. It may even seem like there's no way out.

This problem gets compounded when one starts to project these thoughts into a tainted view of the future. By using past transgressions and pain as excuses not to take action, we do two detrimental things to ourselves.

First, we condemn the future, based only on negative thoughts. We create an impossible scenario for a happy and productive future. Granted, the pain at this point in life might be overwhelming. Did you have a bleak outlook on the future while things were good your marriage?

Hopefully not. Therefore, avoid making decisions about the future based on a very emotional present scenario based on negative past results.

The second problem with this negative feedback loop is that by trying to predict the future – based on the past – the focus is on anything, and everything – *except where you should be focusing your energy.* When something as painful and life-changing as a divorce is occurring, the focus needs to be completely on the present. Concentrate on getting through the problems that need your most immediate attention.

If you feel that because the marriage failed that you will never want to get married again, how does that help you in the present? Since the divorce may not be final, you couldn't get married again immediately. It's just cold logic.

Emotionally, you are not in a good position to be open to dating, so you don't have any marriage prospects. If you haven't physically moved out of the home with your spouse, then where would you and the new bride live?

By taking this logical approach, you are able to come to the conclusion that any thoughts about future marriage prospects, simply have no place in your current thought process. You cannot act on the negative impulse to definitively state that you will not get married again.

PRIORITIZING

Prioritizing your life is the most important step at this point. For now, forget planning your future. You need to delve deep into yourself, to realize what needs to happen right now in your life. Do not look away - go directly into it.

Granted, the temptation to turn away from this seems easy, but this is a type of fear that will only lead you astray. If you try to appease or circumvent the fear, you will never get to the core of your issues and defeat the essence of what is paralyzing you.

Some more examples of your immediate priorities may include: Where am I going to live right now? Do I need to get a divorce lawyer to protect my assets? Will this be an amicable split? The key component to realize is that you need to **focus only on the elements of your life that you truly need to address**.

Long-term goals have no place in your life – *at this time.* Everything needs to happen in stages. Like building a home or an auto engine – if things don't happen in a certain order, the final product will not be of good quality.

Look at this opportunity as a chance to rebuild yourself and your life. You might as well do it the right way and build it in the most solid and durable way possible.

Everything needs to happen in stages.

Later on, we'll explore how to look to the future without living in it. We'll explore more about Prioritizing later. Just let this information settle into your mind.

MARCH 16

A friend's sister told me about a party going on downtown. But with the rain – well, I just didn't feel like driving. Then, the rain let up around 10pm, and I had already bought a Hawaiian shirt – you could dress up as some Creature of the Deep, or do Aloha style attire. Now, I was feeling tired, I needed a shower, and I just wanted to hit the hay.

I just tossed and turned on the pull out couch in the living room that was my bed for the remainder of my duration of the stay in "our" house.

It was the moment of truth – 10:50 PM, either put the head down and sleep or get dressed and head out.

OK, fine, great, let's do it!

Into the shower I headed, and got cleaned up. I put on the Hawaiian shirt – which accentuated my cut triceps – and the sock in the bathing suit, that augmented the Johnson, so it was win-win. All right, so I'm not some Don Juan stud. Anyway, I dressed and was out the door to – where? -- well, I didn't know, but that's half the fun right.

Finally made it downtown, in record time – and parked in Little Tokyo, got the last spot in the lot. All I had were directions to this parking lot from the freeway. Lots of hot women decked out in some wild gear were waiting at the curb. We got into a huge van – the kind that seats 16 people - and were whisked through some of the worst parts of LA, crack dealers – no exaggeration, 'cause one guy who set up the gig told me about six deals he saw that day. Tough area, a warehouse district.

We got dropped off in front of an old building, paid the admission and went in. Beers were $3, and there was music everywhere. I wandered around for almost an hour, taking in the scene, until my friends showed up. We slammed some beers, and listened to the band Mama Sutra. They rocked.

Upstairs was the Raver, dance party stuff. Well, after getting good and loosened up, I busted out on the dance floor. The great part is, you're not really dancing with anyone in particular, yet you're dancing with EVERYONE. I'd take a break and watch the live music going on downstairs.

Women were dancing top-less, at least two with nipple piercings, very exciting. Once dude was dressed up like a lion – complete with mane, and body painted brown. He wasn't wearing a stitch of clothing. No, I didn't stare!

It was decadent, the music was insane, the beat was pumping and everyone was sweating up a storm on the dance floor – very primal and so 'in the moment'. I hadn't been dancing in over five years, gotta do it again soon. I actually only drank four beers the entire night because I was so caught up in the moment.

A little after 5 am, I had enough of all that, so I went home. Not a car on the freeway – and I was in bed before 6 am.

I'd have to rate that bash – definitely one of the top, if not THE top party I've been to. The capper was when I got to my car, and the moon was just off to the side of the tallest building in LA. It illuminated the clouds, and a cool wind was blowing across the town. Yup, it was a great night, and I left before the party got stale.

HAVING FUN WHERE YOU CAN FIND IT

When it was all over with, I found incredible joy in knowing that I had a great time by myself. Granted, I met up with friends there, but for most of the night I partied with strangers I never met.

I found the simple beauty of a full moon as I drove home on the deserted highways. No traffic - in Los Angeles of all places! This wouldn't be the last time I indulged in the basic pleasures. My journey into the depths of my soul was just beginning.

HONESTY WITH THE SELF

There's only one sure-fire way you can get through the forest and into the clear where you can take control of your life. Two words: brutal honesty. You need to be clear about what you are capable of dealing with and what your weaknesses are.

This is not a time to shy away from your shortcomings. This is about opportunity. There will never be another time in your life like this.

It can either be one breakthrough after another, or one continuous meltdown. A difficult situation can be turned to your advantage.

The level of honesty in this arena is different from that in other aspects of your life. The only one that will know if you cheat, is you. This is your time, your life, your issue. Believe that you can make it out alive and in one piece.

> **Breakthrough your pain.**
>
> **Breakdown the situation.**

Trust that you have it within you to make the change necessary to breakthrough. Don't be afraid to lean on others. But, be aware that all the choices you'll make will be yours alone. While you might make poor decisions, at least you can own them.

CONFUSION

There are so many Decisions that you feel you have to make immediately.

How do we divide up our belongings?
What to do about our finances?
Any other joint assets?
Health, auto, home insurance?
Where do I want to live?

This list can go on and on – and certain parts will leap out at you screaming, *this needs immediate attention.*

Start by eliminating the far-reaching future goals and focus on what needs to be done now.

By tackling each Decision individually, you are breaking up the larger problem into manageable units that can be overcome.

PRIORITIZE YOUR DECISIONS

This exercise works in almost any situation.

If you have a large Decision, breaking it down into smaller Elements helps you tackle the problem.

Let's put my life and experience under the microscope so you can make sense of it all.

EXAMPLE

I had several large Decisions facing me head on. I broke them down into smaller units. Out of those realizations, I took the route of addressing the most important Decision.

Decision: Where do I need to live?

I wasn't quite sure that I wanted to stay in Los Angeles. However, I didn't want to commit to moving while I was in such a fragile state of mind. Instead, I chose to push this event to the background.

Decision: What about work?

I took some vacation time that I had accrued.

Decision: Where do I put my stuff?

I didn't have any friends with a garage or basement to put my belongings into. Obviously, I couldn't keep them at my current location, since I was the one moving out. A storage bin offered me a clean and safe place to keep everything I owned.

Now I had a clear goal.

Move my belongings into a storage unit.

I went about completing this process through my Task Management. By asking questions related directly to the above goal, I created smaller Elements. These situations, I could tackle with greater ease.

Element: How do I go about packing?

I bought boxes, tape, bubble wrap and magic markers for this project. I didn't want to be running back and forth to the office supply stores, so I made sure that I had plenty of supplies.

Element: What do I pack first?

Books seemed like the logical choice. I wouldn't be doing any reading in the near future. They pack neatly and since there's nothing to break, it didn't require too much thought to put them into boxes.

Element: How much do I pack per day?

I owned a pick-up truck. I packed up enough to fill the bed of my truck, then drive the load over to the storage bin. If I made one trip per day, I felt that I was making good progress.

Progress leads to success.

As I look back on that time, those days of packing seemed so insignificant. It's pretty basic stuff. At the time, it was a monumental accomplishment for me.

Don't get caught up in how others may view your successes. I probably wouldn't be too impressed by someone who managed to pack their belongings, all by themselves.

Create your own goals, and rejoice when you achieve them. Don't look to others for recognition.

DIAGRAM 4

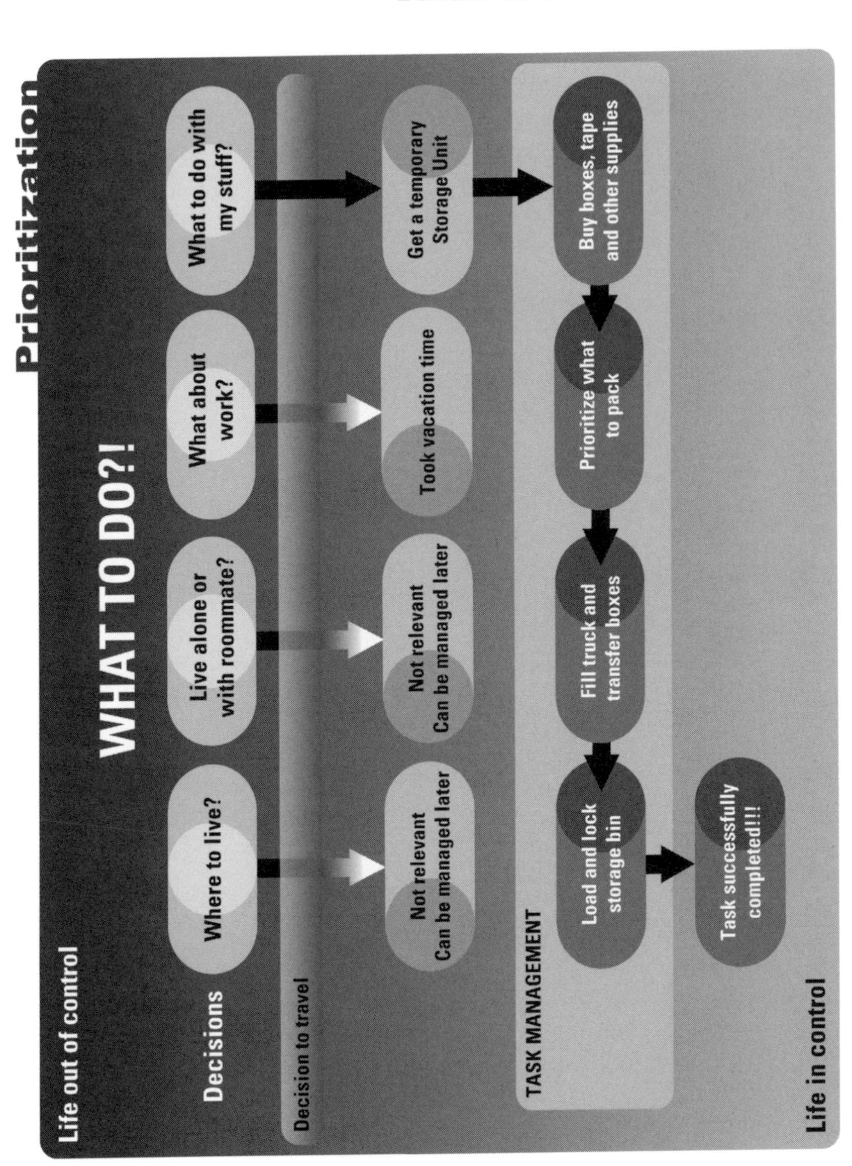
Prioritization
Life out of control
WHAT TO DO?!
Decisions
Where to live?
Live alone or with roommate?
What about work?
What to do with my stuff?
Decision to travel
Not relevant Can be managed later
Not relevant Can be managed later
Took vacation time
Get a temporary Storage Unit
TASK MANAGEMENT
Buy boxes, tape and other supplies
Prioritize what to pack
Fill truck and transfer boxes
Load and lock storage bin
Task successfully completed!!!
Life in control

STATISTICS

"Marriages are most susceptible to divorce in the early years of marriage. After 5 years, approximately 10 percent of marriages are expected to end in divorce – another 10 percent (or 20 percent cumulatively) are divorced by about the tenth year after marriage. However, the 30-percent level is not reached until about the 18th year after marriage, while the 40 percent level is only approached by the 50th year after marriage."

Kreider, Rose M. and Jason M. Fields, 2001, *Number, Timing, and Duration of Marriages and Divorces Fall 1996*; Current Population Reports, P70-80; US Census Bureau Issued February 2002; p. 18

"Compared with unmarried people, married men and women tend to have lower mortality, less risky behavior, more monitoring of health, more compliance with medical regimens, higher sexual frequency, more satisfaction with their sexual lives, more savings, and higher wages."

Bramlett MD and Mosher WD. Cohabitation, Marriage, Divorce, and Remarriage in the United States. National Center for Health Statistics. Vital Health Stat 23(22). 2002 p.3

6

FINALIZE

CUMULATVE EFFECT

All the Elements together had the cumulative effect which satisfied the answer to my Decision. In and of itself, the Decision was too big and vague to effectively be tackled. "Where do I put my stuff" seems like a simple question, but there are many possibilities that are created.

By breaking the question into its component Elements, I was able to chisel away at the Decision and make sense of it.

Notice how I didn't focus on other Elements that did come into play. For a while I was under stress about how I would let all my friends, family and business contacts know about my new address. Where I would ultimately end up living still nagged me, and how I would deal with our mutual friends was a thorn in my side.

All of the above points were important, and absolutely needed to be handled at some point. But they couldn't be tackled until I moved everything I owned out of the house.

Let's look at how various, random Elements can be corralled by finding a Decision that will give the Elements purpose. It's like a solution in search of a problem.

Elements: Why should I get out of bed and face the day? Why bother staying physically active? What's the point of meeting with my friends, since I'll probably be so miserable that I'll bring them down?

Any question that starts with some variation of "Why should I..." needs to find itself a goal, which is the Decision for those Elements.

It was a rather easy answer.

Achieving a state of happiness again was my Decision.

That was reason enough for me to get out of bed, face the day, stay healthy and continue to nurture my relationships with friends.

Later, I will explain how nurturing relationships can actually help you find strength in yourself.

If you have Elements that cannot be connected to a larger goal or Decision, there is still hope.

It may sound like a contradiction, to be using the word "Negative" after everything that has been discussed to this point, but the following is a very positive tool.

NEGATIVE APPROACH

This is a way of looking at a Decision or Element by deciding what you **don't** want.

Upon my return to Los Angeles, I decided to live on my own. I was very clear on what I did not want. I didn't have any friends that I would consider living with. I didn't have family to move in with. I definitely didn't want to live with a stranger for a roommate. All that remained was the decision to live alone. It was the only option that was available to me. It's deciding by default.

I sometimes use this method when I order food at restaurants. If I can't decide what I want, then I decide what I clearly don't want. If I'm not in the mood for Hamburgers, Pizza or Fancy Entrees, then that might leave Salads and Pasta dishes. On further reflection, I might not crave pasta – therefore I am left with Salads by default.

Had I approached the situation with "what DO I want," I may have reached the same conclusion, but it may have taken longer than the Negative Approach.

My time to leave Los Angeles on my journey was on my doorstep. Almost time to walk the talk.

MARCH 23

End game – we're getting there. Almost time to travel.

Coupla' days and we'll be signing our marriage away in front of a lawyer. Kinda depressing – that'll be it, no turning back for either one of us. Though, to be honest, there's no turning back anyway.

Did an extended, angry bike ride. Did about ten miles or so, real heavy winds. But the ocean is soothing, the surf was big, just smashing against the beach – relentless, uncaring, just doing its thing. That's a good way to be, just keep pounding away, regardless of what happens to you, what people think – there's something pure about its consistency. Every day that I go down to the beach – the ocean is still there.

THOUGHT PROCESS 2

So far, we've talked about different thought processes. In reality, nothing thus far has really challenged you. Sure, some of my statements might shock you, but it doesn't really threaten you.

Well, training day is over. Now we get down and dirty. It's time to start applying what we've talked about. At any time, feel free to throw my book against the wall - it's only paper. I only hope that you'll pick it up again and we can continue on.

Whatever you decide, it's your choice.

ACCOUNTABILITY INTRO

At this point, you're going to have to take accountability for why your marriage failed. It doesn't matter if she's the one who called it off. My divorce was against my will, but that is not the point. I had a lot to answer for.

So, grit your teeth, condemn me to the seventh level of Dante's inferno or burn me in effigy. But the failure of the marriage is as much your fault as it is hers.

There may have been actions that you've taken that alienated her. Maybe she felt neglected, unloved, threatened or maybe she was smothered. While it's not necessary to identify what happened, do not fall into the role of the victim. Just accept that she is not the only person responsible for the failure of the marriage.

Do not fall into the role of the victim.

If you dwell too much on the misguided notion that you are blameless, then you are elevating yourself to a god-like entity without flaw. This creates a feedback loop that turns your ex-spouse into an even more horrible person than she actually is.

The process works like this: understand that the marriage is over. Allow yourself to feel betrayed, abandoned or unloved. Now focus on the *possibility* that your actions or inactions were part of the disintegration of your marriage.

Imagine your thoughts as a balance scale. On one side you dump all your negative thoughts. As that side drops, the side you're on rises. By placing some of the responsibility on your side, you allow the scales to come closer to equilibrium.

When you accept your share of blame, you allow yourself to push this part of your life to the background so you can focus on other important issues - such as getting your life in order.

ENTER: THE VOICE

It's amazing what thoughts enter your mind in your deepest moments of stress and desperation. My mind was going into a self-protection mode, and the most random thoughts would pop into my head.

It was looking for answers. The mental Rolodex was being scoured for solutions. I had none. But there was one part of me that kept me going forward.

MARCH 28

The Voice

I've been thinking about why I'm doing this trip. Why take off, with no place to call home that I can settle into, upon my return? Is that really responsible? Am I just running away - most likely, yes!

I should probably be working more. I guess it's because of THE VOICE.

The Voice is this – well, I guess a presence that I have had a few times in my life. The strongest was when I decided to go overseas to Kenya, for a semester of college back in 1988. A truly wonderful, life changing experience. I made friends to last a lifetime – one of them I'll be staying with in NYC this coming Friday.

The voice tells me, in a very powerful way, what to do. When I went to Africa, I knew before I left, before I was even accepted into the school – that a trip to Kenya was the right thing to do.

Right now, it's as if someone is saying – come'on, get on the plane and do the trip, and everything will be just fine.

It's very soothing, very trusting. I guess it's a base instinct, the really deep inner self that's telling you what you really need to do.

I've heard it other times – moving from back east to Arizona, then again when I moved here to LA. But it's the first time I've heard it so strong – as strong as my build-up to the Africa adventure. It's like getting into touch with an old friend. Now I'm wondering, why haven't we been talking lately?

If I could only be in touch with this inner voice all the time, I'd probably be a lot further along in life. Maybe the marriage wouldn't be over. Maybe -- maybe -- maybe. Whatever, you can go crazy with 'maybe'. Do I actively silence the voice, or ignore it? What can I do to nurture it?

In any case, I hope its right about this trip. Nervousness is setting in, but unfortunately, I've talked it up so much, my ego wouldn't let me back out.

If the voice is wrong on this one, then I'll just have to beat the snot out of it. Let's hope this venture into points unknown is the right call.

I was filled with anxiety and self-doubt on a daily basis. It wasn't long after my reconnection with the inner voice, that I started examining what role I played in the demise of our relationship.

ACCOUNTABILITY CONCLUDED

No, we're not done with this point yet.

In my marriage, a destructive event occurred that was left unresolved. I had anger issues. Many times, I would become completely enraged and would be beyond unreasonable. While these outbursts were few and far between, they had a cumulative effect on the marriage.

Think of a relationship as a pillar. Events can reinforce the unity, or chisel away at the base. Nothing I said or did was destructive in and of itself. But over time, the base of the pillar crumbled.

Realizing what cumulative events may have caused the marriage to fail produced three positive outcomes.

First, as I said earlier, two parties create the third entity of the Marriage. By the mere fact that you exist in the marriage, there is a cause and effect within that relationship. It's important to realize that this is not about blame.

If you are driving down the road and are hit by another car, it is safe to say that if you were not in that place at that time, the accident wouldn't have happened.

While you may not be blamed, you need to recognize the fact that because you exist, good and bad things will happen to you. Life doesn't exist in a vacuum.

Second, accepting the fact that your actions or inactions have contributed to the end of the marriage creates an opportunity to change your behavior.

As an example, I wasn't aware of the damage my anger did to my spouse in the marriage. It was my understanding that if a sincere apology was made, and I strove to control my temper, then all was forgiven. This was not the case in our marriage. The cumulative effect was too overwhelming.

If you learn nothing from the marriage, then what is the point of all the pain and suffering? This brings us to the third and final point.

Life doesn't exist in a vacuum.

Commit to applying this learned knowledge in current relationships. This encompasses friends and co-workers, as well as any future intimate relationships.

It's one thing to **learn** by the past, but if we don't **apply** it in our everyday lives, then when gain nothing. The horrible seed of a bitter divorce can still produce sweet fruit that you will enjoy at a different point in your life. It's all how you approach this challenge. Divorce is a difficult wake-up call to receive. Now is an opportunity to wake up and live a glorious and fulfilling life, or stay in the realm of nightmares.

MARCH 29

That Stupid Bluebird

Been a busy week. Getting over a nasty cold, while I get in some work dates. Still making some money at least. Yeah, I was sick, but still able to bike ride and lift. Look at me Jerry, I'm huge! (reference to Seinfeld)

The ex and I got into a 'bit of a row', as the British would say. Yeah, I was probably more sensitive to crud than usual. But hey I can live with that, 'cause I'm a bit touched 'bout the whole divorce thingy. The divorce paperwork was received, signed and mailed back. One more hunk of paperwork will be waiting for me upon my return from Europe and that is that. Done, Kaput, Hasta La Vista.

On the good side of things, there was a woman that I know from work – we always had nice conversations, can honestly say that there never was any flirting beyond, "You look very nice today." In the back of my head, I thought, "You know if I wasn't married, I'd like to hang out with her." I'm not married anymore. I'm not looking for a girlfriend, I just felt that trying to go out and do anything with a member of the opposite sex, kinda goes against the whole marriage thing.

So, we went to a comedy club on Tuesday, saw some great acts. Sat in the front row - little worried 'bout getting picked on, but hey them's the risks. One guy had a bit about using his penis as a catapult to launch cashews into his mouth. It struck me as the funniest thing, I burst out into laughter, so he points to me and says, "Yeah, you gonna go home and try that?" I yelled back, "That's right, tonight!" He tells me not to use peanuts, 'cause they'll hit you in the eye - and goes onto another routine. It was a classy bit of interaction, without actually picking on me.

But today, I was thinking about what I'm going to miss the most. The marriage actually takes second to a bluebird. The neighbor next door used to give him cashews – he moved over three years ago.

I guess the guy at the comedy club with the cashews got me thinking about the bird.

Almost every day I would open the window from the bedroom and this little bluebird would sit on the branch. I'd put two pistachios (unsalted and in the shell) in my hand.

The bird would land on my hand, and take one pistachio – though usually both. I love pistachios because they remind me of the pistachio gelato that I would enjoy with my wife on our annual trips to Italy. The most beautiful country in the world is now going to have bittersweet memories for me.

Anyway, the bird's got this way of shoving the whole shell into his throat – not all the way down, but low enough so that he can hold it in his throat. The other he picks up in his beak. Then he'll fly away.

Some days, he'll take one, fly to the branch, and bust the thing open, eat it, then fly back for the other and go home. Usually we'll go through about four this way. Yesterday – actually there's two, but it's rare the female comes, usually it's the dude – so yesterday, the dude shows up, only he was hiding them all over the place (in tree branches, under the dropped pine needles) and came back about three or four times. We must've gone through eight pistachios. This was definitely a new record. It's like he sensed that I was going away soon.

Whenever he wasn't around, I'd leave them on the sill, but for the most part, he's gotta work for 'em.

The ex isn't as good at feeding him as I am, her hand is small and she freaks out when she feels his tiny talons on her fingers. I told her, if you don't move, he doesn't need to sink them in you – be yielding, yet firm like a branch.

When he lands, he checks you out with one eye, maybe hang for three or four seconds. Then he flies off – I've even gotten to the point where I can sense him spreading his wings, and I give him a little push into the air.

One time, I put the nuts on the dresser, opened the windows and crawled back into bed. I waited, not moving and barely breathing. He flew into the room, landed and hung out for a little bit. There was something magical in seeing such a free creature enter my domain.

Anyway, I never, ever took him for granted. I figured, someday he's gonna die, and I'll never see him again. Or we'd move and not see him. Or in this case, there's no "WE", I am the one moving.

It's coming to an end between us – me and the bird, that is. No more pistachios for this feathered guy, at least not from my hand.

He was a joy every time I saw him, I thought about him from time to time when I'd be out of town – enough to put a smile on my face. Now that I'm leaving for good, I just know that it'll be a little harder this time.

'Cause I'm gonna' miss that stupid bluebird.

7

COUNTDOWN

TRAVEL - AM I SURE ABOUT THIS?

It was time to go, and I mean leave the country. I've been dropping hints about my departure, but here's the real truth as to why I did it. Yeah, it was a form of running away, but my need went deeper than that.

I couldn't stand to be around people who I love and who love me; and agree with me just to make me feel good. I was afraid that leaning on them too much would cause them to see only my side of the story. To let that happen would burden them and would set my misguided course in stone.

Sometimes, unconditional support isn't supportive. During times of crisis, you need someone to slap some sense into you. But it's hard to be that person. I don't know that I could play devil's advocate to a friend going through so much pain.

Second, I needed to get out of town, out of the country, and plant myself into a completely unpredictable situation. I had to know what I was made of, and see for myself if I could survive on an emotional level.

Sometimes, unconditional support isn't supportive.

Out of the frying pan and into the fire, as the saying goes. True, but if you stay in the pan, you know you're gonna die. If you jump into the fire, either you're going to die quickly or you'll find a way to walk across the embers and break free.

By leaving town, I was able to get a view of my life from the outside. I needed to step out of my known world, so I could see what was working, and what needed fixing.

The usual emotional routine would be where I would get depressed about the same issues almost every day. I would face them, deal with them, and get out of my funk. But the feedback loop would repeat itself.

Sisyphus was a mortal in mythology who was doomed to roll a rock up a hill every day, only to have it roll down the hill at night. I was going through the same cycle, having to overcome the same problems everyday.

Meanwhile, there was a whole other set of issues that I had to cope with, but didn't have the chance to address. By leaving the country, I freed myself from the daily, sentimental emotions. By physically traveling to a new area, I gave myself the opportunity to dig deeper into what wasn't working in my life.

Remember that things change - don't take it personally.

APRIL 1

Winding It Down to a Stub

Wow - it's almost time. Can't believe it, I'm heading out in -- well, I'll be at the airport in 48 hours.

I really don't know what to do with myself - I can't really sleep, can't relax, can't watch TV, 'cause I don't pay attention to the images on the tube. One more day of work - then that's it - pack the last of my clothes and head out.

I drove by some lady at a bus stop today, and was reminded of my recent trip to Vegas. I was with two other friends when we were walking to a restaurant to get some burgers.

We were laughing about this and whining about that. Standing at the bus stop was a guy - probably mid-20s.

He was just standing there with a baby in one of those things that straps to your chest, and a blanket wrapped around it.

He loved that kid - would've done anything for it. He may have gotten his girlfriend pregnant, but he was standing by that kid. Something about the way he was holding the baby while it was swaddled in a white blanket, the quilt type that you probably get at Ross for two bucks. The baby was all wrapped up to keep it out of the wind, and his arms were around it - protective. Almost desperate, I mean he woulda held onto that baby to his last breath. Not in a stressed out, fight or flight type of way. Just determined. The way he stared out into the world, it said to me that all he was thinking about was that kid.

My only regret was that I didn't give him cash to take a cab home. It just never occurred to me. Throw him $20, hail a taxi and get him and his kid out of there and into their warm home. Was it some squalid one bedroom, or was he living with his folks, hers? Alone? The three of us kept down our rowdiness and asked him how he was doing as we walked on - no need to set him on edge - after all we were a bunch of hooligans from out of town.

I don't know why I thought about that guy today - but I can't get it out of my head. Maybe because he took his responsibility with his head held high - something I don't know if I could do in the same situation. I'd like to think I could, but with all that's going on with me, I don't even know which way is up.

But that guy did stand tall - and despite everything I've seen in this world - all the successful people I've met - that guy made an impression on me that I'll never forget. I respect him, even though I don't know his name, probably wouldn't recognize him if he were in front of me. I just hope he made it home that night - and that he and the child enjoyed the sleep of the blessed.

I got plans of what I want to see and do - but I know that everything will go to pieces once I hit Europe. Do I really have it in me to slap on the back pack and do it again? Do I have the same fire in my belly to explore the world?

Am I still that take-no-prisoners type of adventurer I once was? I'd like to think so. Only one way to find out for sure.

There's no back up plan, no one to fall back on - no one to rely on. Just me. I'm beginning to feel that crushing burden that no matter what we do, who we talk to or who we spend our life with - we're all really alone on this silly rock. I should find some liberation in that revelation. Maybe realize that there's freedom from responsibility for others. But in the meantime, I only find emptiness. And man, is it vast.

I need to hit the hay if I can get the brain to shut up for a little while. Woulda been nice just to talk to some woman about something - anything. Make me feel alive, perhaps even wanted, desired, cherished. That sounds so pathetic and desperate.

Sleeping on the couch hasn't been too bad - in fact, I enjoy waking up with the sun every morning. I'll miss this house - miss the street, the neighbors, who still don't know I'm leaving. I used to measure my days by the trash pickup - which is every Tuesday. The last pickup that I'll ever see from this house already happened.

I try not to get sentimental - it's bad for the soul. But at the same time - the most important and influential decision of my life -- marriage -- is coming to a crashing halt. In some ways, at least if she died it would be easier. No long good-bye, nor sour memories. For the most part, when people die, you tend to end on a good note. Hey, I wish her no harm, and would be devastated if anything happened to her. Guess I'm loyal to a fault.

Break-ups are like the party that you hang out at just a little bit too long. Better to have the bash broken up by the police at its high point. Then you end with great memories, and the possibilities of just how great the party could've been will always be better in your mind than they could be in real life.

I woke up this morning with butterflies in my stomach - tomorrow I'll probably throw up. I just feel like I have no control over anything.

Well, it's more than a feeling, it's a reality. Except for my motion - which I am exercising by leaving, nothing is within my power.

And my choice of going mobile to another country may be the stupidest thing that I've ever done. Where in the world is the guidebook to tell you what to do in case of a mid-30s break down? I thought I had it all together - when you think that, is when the gods start messing with you - either that or they grant your wishes.

With too much time on my hands, and not enough to do in those final days, my mind was over-thinking things. It was almost time for my departure and my stomach was doing cart wheels. There wasn't much I could do, so I strapped myself in for the ride.

APRIL 3

How to make amends with the future. Profound, huh? Yeah, I'm so deep, gotta make room for all the BS I'm piling up!

My good friend and I went out to dinner after he picked me up at my house. I said good-bye to my ex. I wished her a good life, then left. That was it. Nothing more to say, it was very anti-climatic.

Sitting in the terminal waiting for my flight was the most depressing, lonely night of my life. Here I was, about to hop on a red-eye to JFK, and I was all alone, and it was night. Nobody to talk to, no shoulder to lean on, just me and me alone. With it came a certain amount of peace, which is very strange. I guess it's because all my stuff was locked away in storage and I put all my affairs in order. There wasn't anything left for me to do, except worry.

But worry about what? I was going to visit with a friend of mine, and it wasn't my first time on a plane alone. Once I boarded and got comfortable, I found myself drifting off to sleep. It wasn't the best rest of my life, but at least I was able to leave my troubles behind while the jet ticked off the miles toward my rendezvous with the hardest part of my trip. I was about to be stuck with myself for the next month.

FORGET CLOSURE

Despite what many gurus think about healing from failed relationships, the term **closure** is pure bunk. Life cannot be packed into a closet, with a closed door where you forget about all the emotional turmoil you went through.

If you strive for closure then be prepared for an **opener.**

What if you didn't close things properly - will they resurrect themselves at a future time?

Closure is not, and should not, be your goal. The idea is to live with life as it is played out. It's about neutral acceptance. I didn't receive closure when I signed the divorce paperwork, nor when I moved out. Even now, I still don't feel that I have closure. Life isn't tidy like that.

It doesn't matter that my divorce is still floating around out there, because now I can face it and talk about it without fear or sorrow. Closure is an attempt to lock the skeletons away forever. I prefer to invite them over for dinner to see what they've been up to. My way is better because it works, and all the PhDs in the world won't convince me otherwise.

Even now, I still don't feel that I have closure.

I could go on about this point for another page or so. But I also realize that the person reading this never bothers with the instructions for setting up an entertainment system. So, I'll save the ink and paper.

CASH IN THE CHIPS

Everybody is saving something for the future. Usually it's money. But it could be a generous offer made by a friend. Whatever it is, we all have something in the cosmic bank. When you hit a low spot in your life, such as where you are now, it's time to cash it all in.

There's nothing to save for the future, because if you don't get yourself back on track, you won't have a quality future to live for.

Here's a story I made up that illustrates a tangential point.

A man who lives in a rundown neighborhood decides to write to his congressman, pleading for help. Eager to get re-elected, the politician makes a trip, with his assistants and press in tow.

The man gives the politician a tour of the run-down area, noting several youths hanging around a park.

"All they do is stand around. If we could give them a center where they could be productive, maybe we could put this problem behind us."

Several assistants scribble furiously in their notepads.

He points to trash covering the streets. "More money for garbage collection would help us keep the roads clean."

Again, more scribbling.

They cross the street, and loud music blares from cars parked on the streets. "If we had some more police officers on patrol, they could fine these guys so we'd have a little peace and quiet. Please, we need some help to make this neighborhood inhabitable."

The politician shakes the man's hand and promises to come back with a plan to make things right.

Several weeks later, the politician shows up. The man greets him with great enthusiasm. The politician says, "I've listened to your problems and I have a solution."

He turns to a huge sign being erected in the middle of the park that reads, "No loitering, no littering, no loud music."

...but seriously, I'm here until Thursday; don't forget to tip your bartenders.

What does this have to do with your current situation in life? How many times have we faced dire situations, only to give them a superficial repair? Now is not the time to gloss over the internal problems that you might be facing by going for the "quick fix".

CLEAN UP YOUR ROOM

At first, my whole reason for going to Europe was to get away from everything familiar. A simple change of scenery would give my life a chance to sort itself out. If it were only that clear, concise and easy at the time.

There is also the temptation to use drugs or alcohol to numb the pain as a means to deal with the present situation. After all, if there is no pain, then everything must be working out.

During the six or so weeks that I spent packing up my belongings, I made sure not to ingest anything that would alter my emotional feelings. I was even careful to eliminate the blended coffee drinks that I had gotten addicted to.

But most importantly, I needed to focus on what needed to get done in that exact moment. I needed to be clear on what I wanted to be in my life.

It distilled down to this – do I want to be happy or sad?

If happiness was to be achieved, then I needed to get off my behind and start doing something. There have been many times in life that I've felt overwhelmed, but nothing like this situation. It was in those difficult moments that I realized I needed to clean up my room. It sounds silly, maybe even a bit simplistic, but it always worked.

The state of my room always seemed to reflect my state of mind. Too many bills or useless bits of paper scattered about was always indicative of my thoughts. Chaos. Random magazines needed to be culled, books organized and put on shelves, clothes washed and put away.

Once my living space was cleaned up and organized, I would find peace in my head. This granted me time to clean up my emotional mess.

Let's back up and put together what I talked about earlier.

Before I could really begin to clear up my life, I needed to move out of the house. During one of my therapy sessions, it was suggested to me that I take time off to travel. I've always enjoyed seeing the world, especially visiting my wife's native Italy with her. But for now, that country was off limits to me – I just knew that I couldn't go there, for the happy memories would be too much to bear.

However, travel seemed like a good idea. I didn't have much money, but I knew I could work it out. I structured a block of time in between some of my freelance work. I created a six week window between my departure time and my next scheduled job.

I had been saving frequent flier miles with one of the major airlines for years. Now was the time to cash it in.

There was nothing left to save, this was the moment to start spending – in the financial and the spiritual sense.

What to do upon my return? I had several friends offer me their couches to crash on when I got back. At another point in my life, I would've felt like I was imposing. But with my life in pieces, I was taking them up on their offers. For me, it was simple. I had no other options and if my friends were in the same position, I would want to help them.

If I needed to call them late at night to talk over some things, I did. I got rid of my shame and used every resource available to me to rebuild.

Once I booked my airline tickets, I felt a wave of relief come over me. Until the airline agent told me how much mileage I had, I didn't realize that I had enough for a business class ticket. For once, I was going to travel in style!

Packing was a **cleansing** experience. I was given an opportunity to start over.

Now was the time to get rid of the old. I have always tried to keep things lean, but still, I had an enormous amount of old clothes, dusty files and drawers full of junk.

Everything that went into boxes was stuff I knew I would need and use later on. There wasn't any space for old collections. Sure, I had photo albums and a few sentimental items. But for the most part, if I wasn't using it, I didn't hold onto it.

STREAMLINING

My philosophy hit a snag about halfway through the packing process when I encountered my telescope. For my tenth birthday, my father bought me a beautiful telescope. I used it quite a bit, looking at all the planets, the North Star, the Pleiades, and of course, the moon. I took it with me when I moved to Arizona. The clear, dark skies made for excellent viewing. I would always bring it out at parties to dazzle my friends.

Once I moved to Los Angeles, I never took the telescope out again. The skies were too bright because of the streetlights, and the trees in my neighborhood made it impossible to get a clear view of the heavens.

Here I stood, determined to take only what was essential to me. Everything I owned had to fit into a five foot by ten foot storage bin. It's amazing how quickly it started to fill up.

The telescope was already disassembled and pushed into the back of my closet. What to do? I had already committed myself to a "use it or lose it" scenario. Now I was being faced with a very tough dilemma. Here was a piece of my youth, something that had given me some wonderful moments in my life. How could I get rid of it?

I went for a walk. For me the hardest part was my determination to stick with my process.

Sure, I could keep the telescope and make an exception to my new philosophy.

It's not like anyone else knew the commitment I had made to myself. But I knew I had created such parameters for a reason. This might be the only chance in my life to really remove the materials that had no further purpose in my life.

APRIL 4

I was thinking about the day I parted from a dear friend. Back in the late 70's I really wanted a telescope. See the stars and planets - the pinholes in the curtain of space.

My dad bought me one - it was a six-inch Galileo style - the same type the MAN - Galileo himself used back in the day. That's the diameter of the mirror - six inches not the length of... never mind.

The telescope is a bit bulky, perhaps not as sleek as the stuff out there now. But, I used it in my youth, and through high school and occasionally in college.

With no space in storage, and the uncertainty of where I'll be living next - it was time to get rid of it. I called the local school, and donated it to the Culver City High School.

The principal was ecstatic, the science teacher was in awe, the football team was indifferent. I set it up, gave a teacher the brief run-down of how to use it, then left. That was it, they can find out all the info online. Just take care of it, and don't crack the mirror.

I felt good - sure I miss the big guy, but hey, he wasn't doing what he was made to do - gaze at the stars. I owned him, but never used him. Now, a whole slew of high school kids will hopefully gaze to the heavens. Maybe for one of them it'll be life changing experience, you know, to find a cure for some major disease- perhaps for many, it'll be an excuse to get out of the required Home Economics class - hopefully it will be an excuse for many teens to make out with each other in the darkness. In any case, my work is done, and I've said good-bye to an old friend.

STATISTICS

"In 1996, 60 percent of men and 76 percent of women age 15 and over had been married at least once – 54 percent of men and 60 percent of women had married once, 13 percent of men and women had married twice, and 3 percent had married three or more times."

Kreider, Rose M. and Jason M. Fields, 2001, *Number, Timing, and Duration of Marriages and Divorces Fall 1996*; Current Population Reports, P70-80; US Census Bureau Issued February 2002; p. 6

In 1996, 20 percent of all men had ever divorced, yet only 8 percent of them were currently divorced. Out of the 22 percent of all women who were ever divorced, only 10 percent of them were still divorced.

Ibid; p. 7.

8

LAUNCH

NEVER SAYING NEVER

'Never' is a horrible, dead-end word. It limits the possibilities that life offers in an endless variety of ways.

'Never' shuts down, cuts off and removes elements that make up who we are as humans. But the most damaging thing 'never' does is isolate us from each other.

I picture life as a vast room that I am standing in. During my marriage, a multitude of doors were open to me. There were endless opportunities to grow within the marriage, in addition to my own personal goals.

Once the divorce hit me, I immediately began closing dozens of doors. It's important to know that I alone was responsible for shutting them. The events around me may have been the catalyst to blockade myself from the world, but I am still a creature of my own free will.

I shut down any chance of a future relationship or caring for another person. Even some of my personal dreams seemed out of reach.

As each day went by, I uttered the word 'never' in retaliation to one perceived emotional threat after another. I was saying 'never' to future relationships, intimacy, trust and openness. Since my marriage had failed, how could I ever open myself up to being hurt again?

This is the problem with ignoring the present while being paralyzed by the past.

Suddenly, the room that I lived in that was once big and endless, became small, dark and lonely.

I was giving my ex-wife control over my life. The fact that I was in this painful situation was overwhelming. Here was someone that hurt me badly, yet I was allowing that pain to take over my life. However, I had no intention of going back to this person, even if they tried to make amends. Therefore, I created the perfect, no-win situation. I couldn't be happy without her and I knew I wouldn't be content if we decided to remain together.

Any notion of us reconciling was unrealistic. Energy was wasted even thinking about.

But I was unable to find any happiness or hope in the fact that we were going to be divorced because I closed myself off. Within the parameters that I had set up for myself, I was doomed to misery.

This was a crucial limitation in my life, and one that took many months for me to realize, and ultimately overcome.

It's easy to get caught up in our own logic, no matter how flawed it may seem. By continuing to think in this manner, I was doing myself a grave disservice. I didn't allow myself the opportunity to open up to new possibilities. Instead, I was empowering myself to wallow in my own selfish realm.

It's easy to get caught up in our own logic.

Instead of **protecting** you, 'never' will **prevent** you from healing and moving forward. It's not a shield, but an anchor. 'Never' won't nurture you, but will root you to your grief.

Being scared is never a fun place to be. That's when it's time to go for a stroll, and clear the head. When you're caught up in your feedback loop, just stop thinking. Allow yourself to push the pause button.

RAZOR'S EDGE

The fine line to be walked is the difference between **Selfishness** and **Self Preservation.**

What exactly is that point? It isn't precise. The litmus test for this line in the sand has to do with why you're cutting yourself off from certain emotional responses.

Are you consciously working through what has to be done, or are you in denial?

I crawled into my cave many times. When I found that I was sleeping too much, my actions became purely Selfish. My long hikes and bike rides were my acts of Self Preservation.

In both cases, I removed myself from the core of my pain (i.e. my divorce and all its subsidiaries).

The issue isn't one of avoidance. Are you avoiding it by staying in your closet, or are you getting out in the world? Doing something – anything – out of the house is a step forward to your healing process.

If you've spent several days in the living room, clad in sweat pants, without a recent shower and having pizza delivered; you need to change your routine.

Just getting out to a park or a nice drive can be therapeutic. Take in some beauty.

APRIL 10

So, a couple nights ago, I flew in on a red-eye into JFK. At least I slept some because the seats were comfortable. I grabbed my luggage and took a shuttle to my friend's house out on Long Island.

I know Bob from a study overseas program in Kenya that he and I were on, back in 1988. We've kept in touch over the years. What'd we do? Well we hung out and just talked. Actually, I didn't dwell too much on my divorce.

He's a good cook, so we went shopping to some of the various specialty stores near his house. The trip gave me a chance to ground myself.

I was able to spend time with someone who knew me rather well, yet wasn't around me every day. We were able to talk about new developments in our respective lives.

I went into the city for a day, and saw another friend. Even though it was raining, I still enjoyed the adventure, and walked my feet off.

But last night - wow! What a day - it all just fell together. Saw a friend's house out in Coventry - what a masterpiece. Post and Beam construction. Absolutely gorgeous. He designed it and did most of the construction himself.

Came back home - dinner with some family. Got a phone call from my nephew who was hanging out in Hartford. I was dropped off - no ride home, oh well, time to wing it. Two very close friends from my childhood were in town. They were my second family when I was in high school. I remember that their mom even made me a cake from scratch on my 21st birthday.

It was great seeing them. Someone familiar, friends from the past. Didn't talk about my divorce at all, for one day it didn't even cross my mind. Crashed at my nephew's apartment that night, took him to breakfast the next day – then he dropped me off at my Mom's. An absolutely exciting - wonderful day. No, I can't let it go at that.

It was one of the best days I had in a very long time. Without any expectations of anything going right, things just fell into place and I was invited along for the ride. Makes me smile just thinking about it.

My load had lightened for a day because I finally surrendered to the bad events that were occurring in my life. I was so tired of fighting what was going on, that I gave up. I didn't give up on myself, just on the senseless battle. Who or what was I struggling against? It was really my attempt to hold on to how my life used to be. By going with the flow, things fell into place.

I took up many fruitless battles time and time again. It was only when I dropped my defenses that life showed its gentle side. This feeling of euphoria didn't last that long, though.

I thought the loneliness that hit me at the airport in Los Angeles was horrible. Nothing compared to my emotional rollercoaster as I was about to embark on the overseas part of my journey.

It was one thing to be around family and friends. Now, I was about to go to a place where nobody knew me.

APRIL 14

Right now, I'm at JFK, inside the airport business center. I've never been more scared in my life. Not sure what it is. I'm not afraid of flying, I'm just very lonely. I feel lost - not sure where I am, or where I'm supposed to be. There's simply no grounding in my world. Now, I'm trying to put a happy face on things. But darn it, I am simply petrified.

This whole deal of going to Amsterdam just wasn't a good idea - now my backpack is on the plane, and I'm stuck. Maybe it has to do with not having a place to go home to. I just don't know.

I wouldn't know where to go - even if I blew off this trip, would I go back to LA? I'm in an airport bursting with people, and I'm the loneliest guy on the planet. I feel so sick to my stomach, I can't even cry. Perhaps if I did, I'd feel better about things.

On the way down to New Haven to catch the bus to the airport, I went by two tall radio antennas out in West Hartford. When I was a kid, I'd look out my bedroom window and see them way off in the distance, their lights blinking off and on in the night sky. I wondered what was beyond them - what lay in store for me. Like a big goalpost, pointing the way to a new future. There were some antennas west of Boston that I could see from my dorm in college - same feeling. It was like they were a gateway to something else.

Well, I've been somewhere else. I met my wife somewhere else. I moved somewhere else. I don't know if the 'somewhere else' route is the best way to do this, I don't know what to do.

I had a bad dream last night - normally I never dream about other people, but this nightmare was that my ex was in trouble. Very disturbing. I called her, she's fine, but why the dream? Why can't I get a grip on my emotions and just look forward to this trip? I try so hard to be in the moment, for good or bad. But I can't shake this sadness. Maybe it was because I was around my family - who were incredibly supportive. Maybe that's why I haven't had to face the real pain yet. I just don't know.

More questions than answers. What will tomorrow bring - how will I feel when I get there? Will I wimp out and take an early flight home? My anxiety attacks are getting bad. I'm doing the deep breathing and all that crud, but it just doesn't ease the pain. I was hoping each day would get a little better - a little easier. But it's not. Do I still love my ex - or am I falling back on what is familiar? I miss everything about her - watching her when she sleeps, eating dinner - all the little things I miss are too painful to think about because it reminds me of what I had - and lost. And will probably never get back.

Healing is going to take a long time - I got time - but not the time to wait it out. If only I had done things differently - maybe I wouldn't be so jammed up mentally.

I hope staying at the hostels is good - I'm doing it because it'll be easier to meet people, more of a laid back experience.

I remember my first sleepover - it was two houses down, and I got so homesick, that my mother picked me up at midnight. I feel exactly that way now - only what I am I homesick for? I don't have a home.

It's a big world out there - I just don't ever remember it being so lonely. I need to accept that fact that I am alone. We came into the world alone, we'll all die alone. I was just hoping to fill the time in between with someone I could love, and who would maybe love me back. Is that asking for so much?

EVEN WHEN LIFE SUCKS, BE HAPPY

You'd think somebody going on a trip to Europe would be happy. Most people only get a couple of weeks off a year. When they do get vacation time, they can't hop on a plane overseas. I had the opportunity of a lifetime and I could only complain.

I knew at the time that I was being a bit ungrateful, but I couldn't find a way to be happy. It's the person, not the situation that creates happiness.

I like to use this example to illustrate my point.

Inside a car are two identical twins. Both of them are sitting in the front: one is driving, the other is a passenger. For you analytical types out there, they both went to the same schools, played the same sports, and were both equally loved by their parents. In other words, these two people are as identical as two humans could get.

The car is stopped in New York City traffic. Nobody is moving. The man who is driving is completely happy, while the passenger is tearing his hair out. How can that be? They are both essentially the same person, in the exact same vehicle, both sitting in front and are in the same situation. Why are they having different emotional responses?

The one driving is the limousine chauffeur. He's getting paid whether or not the passenger gets there on time.

The passenger is running late for a very important meeting.

They have separate responses to the same events. Therefore, it's the person and how they interpret the events around them, not the events themselves that shape their happiness or misery.

Let's continue forward, because the only way out of this forest is to keep walking. You may hit a few more dead ends like I did. But keep moving.

YOUR SPOUSE MIGHT NOT HAVE IT SO EASY

This may cause an incredible amount of anger, sadness and hate - either towards her or towards me. It's OK if that's how you feel. Have a temper tantrum, just don't hurt anybody or yourself.

When I first understood that my wife no longer wanted to be with me, I was devastated. I quickly spiraled downwards, because in my mind, I was convinced that she was having an easy time with this decision.

This was a belief that I firmly held, which validated my negative feelings towards her and my resentment towards the whole sacrament of marriage. It empowered me to feel bitter and cemented my righteousness for nurturing my hatred. The reality of the situation was that she didn't walk away emotionally unscathed.

I know this from brief conversations we had upon my return from Europe, and from our mutual friends.

What this bitterness did was spread the gap between my sorrow and my ability to find happiness again.

Every day, the goal of feeling good about me felt further away. In my mind, she was having the time of her life and had no demons to battle.

This is illogical. Have you ever been in a job or situation where you've been replaced or fired? It doesn't feel good.

Flip the situation, have you ever been in the position of having to tell someone that they no longer have a job? Unless you really had it in for that person, you probably didn't feel so good that night either.

Stop trying to compare your level of suffering to others or to your spouse. It shouldn't matter to your goals, only your survival is important.

RIGHTEOUSNESS IS WRONGHEADED

Right now, you might be stuck in some swampy mess in the middle of this forest. Maybe everything is starting to look more like a jungle. Either way, you have it in you to get out of this mess.

It's easy to get sucked into righteousness even in the most negative of times. Magnifying this problem can be well intentioned friends that listen to your issues and validate your feelings. During a time of crisis (remember, this isn't necessarily a negative word), people who love and care for you tend to – well – just listen.

They may shy away from challenging your beliefs, as a way of supporting you. But instead of helping you, it may allow you to etch your negative feelings in stone.

That's why I needed to leave the country for a bit.

Use this time to dive deep into yourself and get to the root of why you are feeling so confused and hurt.

My belief that my ex-wife was emotionally unscathed allowed me to remain in my own negative frame of mind. I had complete justification for my feelings.

Use this time to dive deep into yourself.

Once the fog lifted from my mind and I could see that she was having trouble coping with her own problems, it rocked my world. Now I had to deal with the fact that others were suffering as well. Suddenly, the whole world didn't revolve around me. Other people had feelings as well.

When I was able to accept this fact, then I could begin taking responsibility for my role in the marriage. Maybe I wasn't the victim I thought I was.

Getting to this point was the hardest struggle I had ever undertaken. It wasn't until I reached this breakthrough that I was truly free, and able to redirect my life.

Unfortunately, I didn't discover this point until well after my return from Europe. I bring it up now, so that you can use it as beacon to help guide you.

I knew I was going to miss certain things about being married. Perhaps I was more invested in the concept of being married than the marriage itself. Being a couple can be very cozy; you're invited to other events with other couples. Two is a nice, even, happy number.

One can be lonely, but isn't always so. Three is an odd number, someone is left out, unless you're the minority in a ménage e trios.

I knew my life wasn't going to be the same. I was never going to sleep in our bedroom again, or hang out in the living room with her, watching TV. There were a lot of things that I was going to sorely miss.

I gave myself permission to stop thinking about memories that would make me sad. I was on an overseas trip - I had to find a way to enjoy the moment.

STOP TALKING AND START DIGGING

While you're going through your divorce, try not to tell everybody about what is going on inside you.

Now, that's got to be raising a red flag inside you. The only way out of this mess is by talking about it, right?

Well, that's not completely true.

Talk about your issues when a new blockade comes up. Like when you've hit a snag in your life and you don't know how to get around it.

You cannot talk about your divorce if you're only playing the same record over and over. When I was first going through my problems, I would tell any and everybody what I was feeling. After a few weeks, I realized I could tell my story without thinking about.

It was like somebody hit a selection on a jukebox. I wasn't speaking from my heart, but from memory. Eventually, I could talk without really listening to myself.

This is bad for two reasons. First, it didn't give me the opportunity to explore if I really felt the same way. For a few weeks, I hadn't reflected on my emotions. Was I still incredibly hurt and angry, or was it just a mantra?

Second, if I was still in the same negative place, then I had to do something to get myself out of there. At some point, I needed to break the cycle of despair to reach a point of happiness.

Sounds good in theory, but I wasn't there just yet.

APRIL 15

I'm here, so what?

Big friggin' deal, Amsterdam - never thought I'd hear me say that. But it's just not what I expected. Maybe the whole dealio of traveling has just soured for me. I don't know. Most people would give their left and/or right arm to do a trip like this - and all I can do is whine. Me and my big stupid problems. Pathetic, ain't it? Yeah, I'm disappointed in me too. Stop the whining and enjoy the trip. Wish it were that easy - I really thought I could switch things off and just have a blast. But no, not right now.

It was at this juncture in my life that even I was getting tired of me. Something had to change. The world was as it always was, so I had to be the one to alter my attitude. The choice was completely up to me.

The hostel I stayed at was comfortable enough, but not nice enough that I wanted to hang out in my room all day. I walked the streets, got something to eat, took pictures and even did a boat tour. The change in scenery was just what my battered emotions needed.

Even I was getting tired of me.

APRIL 16

AHHHHhhhh Amsterdam!

Cool, feeling much better today. I was walking around town, taking in the spring like atmosphere until midnight last night. It was my first full day in town, and jet lagged or not, I tore it up! There was a beer garden in a nearby park. Must have been about 150 people hanging out and enjoying the night. There were up lights in the trees highlighting the new buds. Should have brought shorts – it was in the 70s today - and I packed a sweater, hat and gloves!

Got some fries, visited the various places - museums and other cultural meccas - of Amsterdam. Gorgeous weather, and the women here are very attractive, in a Nordic sense.

I'm sharing a room with five guys from Spain. Really nice - hardly ever there. When they do go out, it's all for one and one for all! We got lock boxes under the bed, I can fit my entire backpack in there, so my stuff is safe.

I leave for the Beach on Friday at 8pm, I may hop on a train and go out of the city tomorrow - not sure. Need to get train schedules 'cause I'm going to Cologne from the Beach hostel.

Having a better time - it just hit me this afternoon as I was gazing at the view of the park from the balcony in my room - "You know what - you're in Amsterdam, think you can just try to enjoy it?"

Yeah, that I can do!

9

KNOCKED OFF COURSE

FRYING PAN

When I understood that I was in a hot pan, I decided I had to jump out. Since I couldn't retreat, I figured I'd either meet my doom or salvation soon. There's a time and place to say good-bye to negative emotions in your life. I was ready to start right then and there.

I realized after writing in my journal that I was miserable when I had too much time alone to think. Sampling new experiences kept my mind sharp and challenged me.

The morning I was leaving for the bus to JFK was one of the worst days of my life. I was in a horrible place. My nerves were shot, and realized I was going on a trip to lands I had never been to before.

In the end, it all worked out. I just needed to takes things slowly. I figured out how to handle the challenges that were directly in front of me.

After getting on the airplane to Holland, I knew that things were out of my hands. Life was going to happen, I just needed to show up. Amsterdam offered me distractions, so I didn't have time to wallow in my misery.

I went with the flow when I met up with my friends and nephew that one day. I was willing to try it again.

APRIL 17

Whew - another exhausting day stumbling 'round Amsterdam.

Ate at FEBO - it's like an automat - put your coin in the slot - 'bout $2 - and you get a sandwich. They're in a window, so you can see what looks good. 'Course all the sandwiches have a bite taken out of the back, where you can't see it, but they still taste good.

I'm settling into a decent routine - waking up at 10am, stay up until 2am. Lot's going on at the hostel.

Went to the Central Train Station to get some information on the trains into Germany, it's a huge building with its back against an enormous canal. From there, the city goes out like spokes on a bicycle wheel, only it's half a wheel. There are smaller alleys that connect the major spokes. That's where all the fun stuff happens! The canals go through the city, like concentric horseshoes, with the station in the center.

So many bikes, the one-speed kind with fenders to keep the water off you. People are all dressed up, suits, dresses - this is how they get around.

Very stylish ride, and Amsterdam is very bike friendly.

There's so much to see. Just taking in the architecture and smelling the scents wafting out of restaurants is a real joy. If I lived here, it would probably be just another day. But for me, it's a new awakening!

Soon, I'll be leaving the Netherlands - well not tomorrow- but if I don't get moving – like zoinks (Scooby Doo reference), I'll be leaving almost one week after I got here. Probably have to scratch Budapest - want to see the Rhine and Vienna - gotta see Prague - don't know, but for some reason I'm really drawn to that city. We'll see how it goes - and how much time I want to spend on a train.

Oh, almost forgot about the cobblestones in the street. This one guy was telling me that the previous night, the whole street was dug up.

They get a back hoe to pick up the cobblestones by scraping them just underneath the surface. Then they go to work with their digging and replacing whatever is broken. They'll lay the cobblestones back down - dump dirt on it, to keep it in place - put a street sweeper over it, to clean up the excess dirt, and the cars end up packing it down.

No concrete, mortar or tar. Very replaceable, flexible in the terrain and easy to remove. If you went out to one of the streets, you might be able to pry one up.

Well, at least I thought it was neat.

Amsterdam was rubbing off on me. I was able to relax and forget my old self for a little while. I walked until I felt like passing out so that I'd fall asleep upon arriving back at the hostel.

During the train rides through the city, I was trying to find a new way to connect with other people while still allowing myself to be protected from emotional harm.

This is what I came up with.

BARRIERS vs. BORDERS

In life, it's important for people to set up different ways of protecting themselves from being emotionally injured from others. There are different degrees of protection, ranging from wearing your heart on your sleeve to being a closed off hermit.

Somewhere in between there is a balance to be had.

Barriers involve putting up rigid parameters as a means of emotional protection. This can take the form of non-social interaction (being a wall flower) or simply not opening oneself up to intimacy in any form (not dating).

Think of the **Barrier** as a rigid, immovable structure that keeps you completely isolated.

The problem with any Barrier is that it prevents you from having the opportunity to really connect with anyone else, just as you rob them of getting to know you.

Protection is assured, since you have put up a front. You don't let others in. Think of the gumshoe detectives in movies that remain an enigma to the woman who loves them, yet they cannot love back.

The healthier way to protect yourself, is to set up a series of **Borders**.

Think of a map of the United States. One can cross the Borders between states with ease. There may be slight changes in local laws or speed limits, but for the most part, one wouldn't know they are in a new state if it weren't for a signpost.

Barriers are more like the Cold War era Berlin Wall. Huge, concrete structures designed to intimidate in the name of protection. They are often impermeable - nothing goes in or out.

While they might offer a certain degree of protection, they come at a very high cost. Usually, there's a lack of social interaction with other people in the world.

Barriers offer no opportunity to reconcile with the past by offering a chance of having a productive and loving tomorrow. They only exclude others from your life. In the process, they tend to imprison you to a life of unhealthy solitude.

Utilizing the Borders method doesn't mean that you have to open yourself up to pain and suffering. Rather, it gives you a set of guidelines for you and others to follow during social interactions. This encompasses a wider range of relations other than just intimacy. It is good to set up Borders with friends and family.

Remember the cobblestones in Amsterdam? Think of your Borders as stones that are arranged in such a way that they can be moved around, without sacrificing strength. The cobblestone roads are just as strong as asphalt.

But when you have to move them to get at the surface below, it doesn't make such a mess.

Another way to look at this concept is like a knight's armor. With plate armor, he might have better protection, but will sacrifice the mobility of chain mail. Flexibility over rigidity allows you to adapt quicker to your environment.

Below are some simple examples. Although they might be extreme, the answers illustrate the differences between Borders and Barriers.

BARRIERS vs. BORDERS EXAMPLES

1. A friend comes over to your house and constantly eats your food. You're tired of him emptying your refrigerator. How do you react?

Border – Tell him to knock it off, or put some price tags on the food and tell him you'll start charging him every time he wipes out your cold cut drawer.

Barrier – Kick him out of your house, and never speak to him again.

2. You go out on a date with a woman who you met through a friend. You thought there might be something there, but she doesn't return phone calls. What should you do?

Border – Don't move so fast at first, lower your expectations on where you see the relationship going. Just enjoy the moment.

Barrier – Why are you dating? Get back to your apartment/house/friend's couch and swear off women forever!

3. A person at work has a habit of saying things that embarrass you whenever there's a large group of people around. How do you handle this?

Border – Tell him/her in private that you don't like the games they're playing. If they continue to do it, you'll simply make sure you're not around them when other workers have gathered. You'll also make it a point to make sure the other workers know why you avoid him/her.

Barrier – Quit your job and stay home.

These examples illustrate that when it comes to confrontation, we have choices. We can avoid the people or the uncomfortable situation altogether. Or, we can confront the issue and find ways to protect ourselves, without becoming isolated.

A person cannot take advantage of you, if you don't let them. Same goes for others that hurt you. I was so wrapped up in protecting myself that I found myself shunning others for fear of criticism about my failed marriage.

My trip to Europe forced me to be more outgoing; otherwise I was doomed to a journey of solitary grumpiness.

APRIL 18

Remember how I was praising FEBO - well I got two more sandwiches on my walk - they're good, all lightly fried - chicken, fish, miscellaneous. Sure, it felt good last night - but about 8am I was awakened by a rumbling in my gut -- deep within. I won't go into detail, but if there was a klaxon in my stomach - that baby would've been at full volume.

So much for FEBO, too much of a good thing.

Overall, I have been eating well, lots of yogurt and tons of fruit. I've been slamming about two liters of water each day, from all the walking. With the exception of last night, I haven't had too much beer.

So, how's the Flying Pig - my hostel? Cool, there's breakfast every morning - toast and a hardboiled egg - you get there after 10am, nothing is left and breakfast is over by then anyway.

They've got a bar downstairs where people can drink and smoke. I can't stay long - I don't like smoke – and the tobacco just gets in all your clothes and your hair, they don't really have any ventilation down there. It's cool, but in small doses - like your local dive. The bar at the hostel is really safe, people are friendly. It's easy to strike up a conversation with anyone because we're all fellow travelers.

That's the purpose of the hostel, to meet people. I'm just chilling out with a cappuccino, before I head to another park - my feet are tired, and I need a nap. I hit the ground running, and I know that I'm acclimated to the time, that's no big deal. But the late nights, and getting woken up by my Spanish roommates in the wee hours - man, it's like being in a college dorm.

At the hostels, some dorms fit 20 people, that's too big for me. No thanks. I booked both beds in the double room at the beach, just so I can lay out my stuff. I feel secure when I lock stuff in my trunk, problem is, I don't want to have to lock it up all the time, let me lock up the room.

Isn't the purpose of this trip to find out where I want to live? LAX, PHX, BDL, BOS - I'm still no closer to figuring that one out. Yeah, I got a place to crash when I get back, but no place to call home. Weird. But I'm hoping to find a way to get through it all.

INNER STRUGGLE

I was still struggling with myself. Even though I only had a backpack and a small day pack for my camera and reading material, I was carrying enough emotional baggage to warrant a porter.

There weren't good days and bad days. That was looking at too large of a picture. I had good hours and bad hours. My emotional swings were that erratic. Something as simple as getting bumped on the sidewalk or watching a couple hold hands could set me off.

When I was feeling angry at the world, I would just keep walking. Before the end of the trip, I wore through a new pair of shoes. The pavement bore the brunt of my anger.

APRIL 19

So, here I am in Norddwijk (Nord-wide) after visiting Leiden (Lie-den) They had a couple of working windmills, that's right, they reclaimed all their land from the sea - not to mention the Dutch Trading Company - great ship building, and the earliest sewage system in all of Europe. Not a bad group of people; very smart with great engineering skills.

Walked the canals - did you know that they have canals here? In Holland of all places! There was an outdoor market. Food, clothes, pretty much everything was for sale. Ate on the run again - saw some parks and a few churches. They really love their greenery here in Holland. Lot's of open spaces, very flat. Veeeerrrrry Flat.

Woke up this morning with the usual argument with myself. Should I stay or should I go?

Part of me is saying:
-- The trip isn't going as expected.

The other part says:
>>> Well, what did you expect?

-- Well, not this!
>> Great that's just great, I need this.

-- Don't get upset!
>> I'M NOT....I'm not upset. What do you want from me?

-- I just thought it would be -- you know.
>> No, that's the problem I don't know.

-- Well, didn't you think it would be different?
>> No, 'cause I wasn't really expecting anything - see it's a vacation, right? Besides you think anything will be better if you just go home? You don't even have a home.

-- No need to get nasty.
>> Nasty? I'm pointing out a fact, you twit! Look, we're here, it costs money to change the ticket, and I'm sure that some landscaper working from 5am until 7pm at night to feed his family and put a roof over their head is really going to be sympathetic with your plight. Boo Hoo, lookit me, I'm in Europe and unhappy. Shut your pie hole!

I swear, next time I go on vacation, I'm leaving myself at home - sometimes I can't stand me. Granted, I have a few valid points, but even the worst day here has to be better than being in LA - I mean, it's a great place to be homeless!

The buses are very well organized, took it into Leiden - as I said. Great weather - a bit brisk, glad I brought the jacket and sweatshirt - finally! Spent about 4 hours there - it's a 30 minute ride - and I already bought my train ticket to Cologne. Leave Monday - hope the buses run then. Monday is also a holiday.

No clue what I'm doing tomorrow. Seems like I've been alone a lot on Easter. But, I was also in Italy with my ex-wife's family, several years ago. Most of the stuff'll be closed, so I'll figure I need to find something to do. For now, time for a beer!

SENSE OF PLACE

In order for me to have gotten in touch with myself at that point in my life, I needed to understand my Sense of Place.

Place is an emotional state – the awareness of being that one may or may not have right here and right now.

It is irrespective of the physical place. The reason why this distinction is important is that no matter where you are physically, the emotional sense of Place will remain the same.

I visited with my family shortly after my divorce to try and find a sense of grounding in my life.

I believed that if I went back to my roots and visited my childhood stamping grounds, I could rebuild my life from ground zero.

It didn't work out as I expected. The physical place was the same, but I was not. Sure, the trees, the old neighborhoods, the hangouts I spent countless hours with friends – those were all still there.

But they weren't exactly the same. Some restaurants were under new ownership, fresh coats of paint covered the walls, the streets were widened in some areas, the same houses still stood, but the families I knew had since moved.

The basic veneer of my physical world was still intact - buildings, streets, and trees. But upon closer inspection, intangible elements were forever changed.

Putting the focus on myself, I had changed. Granted, people recognized me. This became perfectly clear when I went to the supermarket.

There, I ran into a Mr. G. As a child, I played in the tree house that he had built for his son, Todd. He and I were best friends from Kindergarten through third grade.

While playing at their house on an otherwise good day, I slipped while climbing out of the tree house and broke my arm just above the wrist. After a call to my mother, a trip to the hospital and a cast put on my arm, Mr. and Mrs. G visited my home that night to see how I was doing.

I was a child and they were concerned that all was well with me. I'll never forget the look on their faces – one of concern and pain for what I had gone through.

On this particular day, over twenty years later, we were standing several feet apart when I went up to him. He didn't recognize me at first, until I told him my name. Suddenly, we were whisked back in time. I was the young, fearless kid tearing up the neighborhood with his son. We shared some laughs and talked about that fateful day.

Then we talked about his retirement. I gave him the brief rundown of my life. Todd was grown up, had his PhD, and was expecting his first child in the next few weeks.

All of us were older and we had been through many life-changing experiences in those twenty-something years.

Although we were different, we were both talking together, sharing a common bond that was forged in the past. Just like so many other connections that I had created.

It was then that it hit me. I didn't really go home to find security in the past. I went home to learn how to live in the present. The veneer that I had expected to find solace in was a fantasy in my head. It was **Nostalgia** – and at this point in my life, this was a dangerous area to be exploring.

By wading into these waters, I was trying to create a safety net that no longer existed.

FORGET NOSTALGIA

Nostalgia is defined as "A longing for something far away or long ago or for former happy circumstances."

By breaking down this definition, we can see the destructive properties of Nostalgia that can anchor us in the past – and not in a positive manner.

I went home to learn how to live in the present.

Explore the word "longing." It has such a lonely connotation – as if one is concentrating on the emptiness of the now by trying to reach for something "far away or long ago." It's the complete denial of everything that life is giving to you in the moment.

Think of our existence as a lavish dinner. Life is offering the very best that it has, right in this moment. But focusing on a meal we had in the past denies us the privilege of nurturing ourselves in this moment. How can anyone shake his hunger if he refuses to partake in the feast before him?

"Happy circumstances" is a term that gives me the most trouble with nostalgia. When we root our happiness in the past, we usually overlook the sour aspects of our life.

The people or events that hurt us tend to go away, and everything seems much prettier. Even now, when I talk about my trip to Europe, I usually recall the happier moments. It isn't until I really concentrate on the day-to-day routine I underwent that I begin to re-live the loneliness and uncertainty.

There is pain and suffering in everyone's past. In one aspect, it is important to focus on what is good. If we dwell too much on the pain and suffering, we haven't learned from our mistakes or transgressions that have been either inflicted or received.

However, we shouldn't view our lives through rose-colored glasses. By denying the pain we have experienced, we can diminish the episode as a whole. When looking to the past, maintain a balance by looking for the positives, without forgetting the negatives.

Here's a riddle for you. How far can you walk into a forest?

The answer is, halfway. After that point, you're walking out of the woods. So, the good news is, at some point you'll be halfway through your journey. The bad news is, you don't know where the halfway point is until your journey is over.

Right now, you are more than halfway through this book!

10

TROUBLE SHOOTING

REMEMBER SYNTHESIS?

Every day we make decisions that affect our lives. By reflecting on those options and understanding the outcomes that resulted from them, we can bring decision process into one, present occurrence. From that derives a new, positive outcome by using Synthesis, which is a way to truly be in the present, while keeping an oblique eye on the past and present.

Focus specifically on the **choices**. If you concentrate on the **outcome** of those decisions too much, it may paralyze the thought process. Why? Because then the focus is on, "Will this action result in a similar, negative outcome?"

It's important to remember that this isn't about judging our past choices. Our goal is to establish a better thought process. Even though the choices we face today may be similar to the choices from the past, the outcomes will be vastly different.

When I was deciding where to live, I realized that travel would be the best decision. Upon reflection, I decided to travel to Europe and visit some countries that I hadn't before.

By looking at the string of choices I made, I was able to design a new way to make my decisions and create **Opportunity** in my life.

DIAGRAM 5

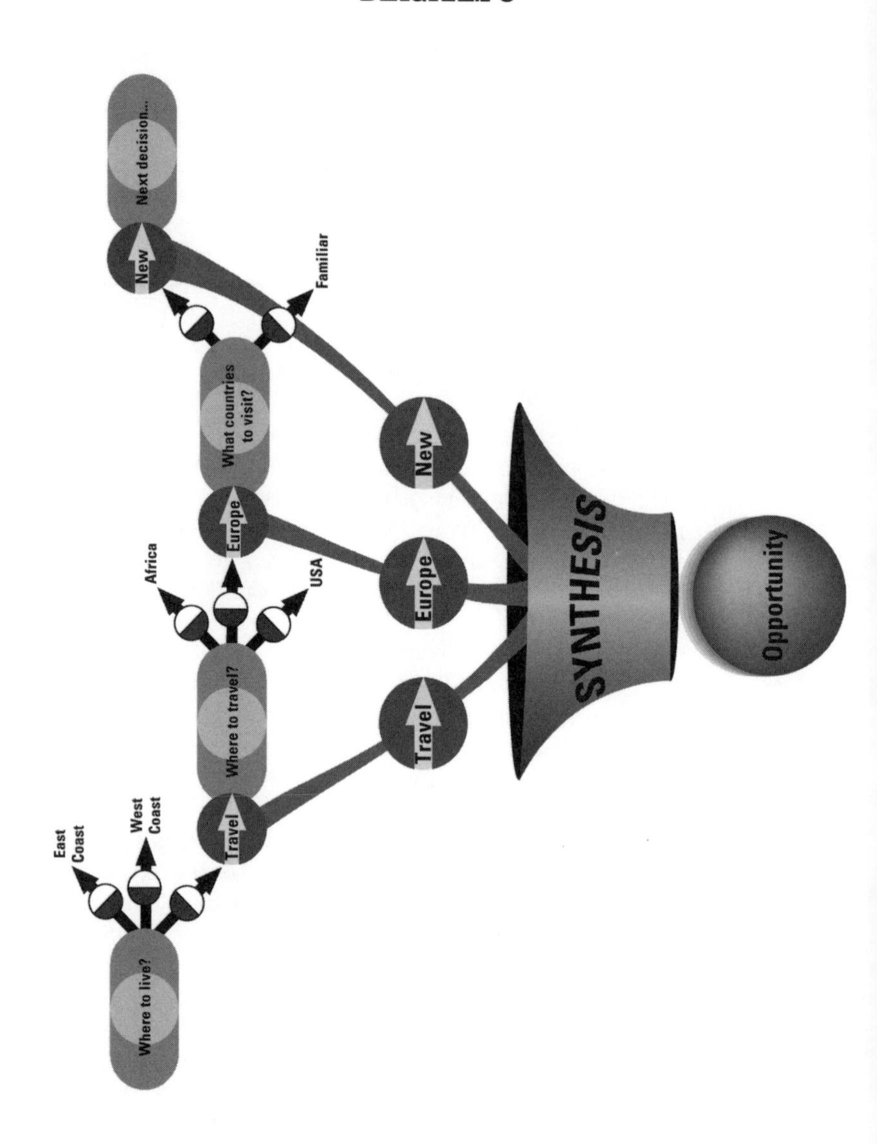
Where to live?
East Coast
West Coast
Travel
Where to travel?
Africa
USA
Europe
What countries to visit?
Familiar
New
Next decision...
Travel
Europe
New
SYNTHESIS
Opportunity

NOSTALIGIA REVISITED

Nostalgia compares the past with the present. Depending on how the approach is made, the present doesn't stand a chance. This is because the past is the benchmark that the present is stacked up against. When one compares, one has a certain expectation of an outcome.

When I was visiting my family, I drove around town. I couldn't help but feel sad that all I had were memories of places I once played and visited. Coupling this with my recent divorce, I sunk into a deeper sense of despair.

My going home only drove me further into sadness. There had to be a way to turn this around. I quickly realized that I was caught up in the Nostalgia. My comparisons offered me no possible way to accept what the present was presenting me. In life, the possibilities are endless.

Instead of seeing an apple orchard that was decimated by a new housing community, I saw beautiful homes. Each one was different from the rest, not a cookie-cutter development.

Outside, a new generation of children played, able to experience all the joys that life had to offer. Even though some of the fields held shopping malls, the river that I would skip stones across was still there.

The new supermarkets built on the edges of town brought together people from all over. At the deli counter, I ran into the parents of more of my friends. People were friendly as I passed by them with my shopping cart. In the end, the old Mom and Pop grocery store that is still near my mother's home does a solid business.

The old hardware store that was expanded and lost some of its character was still operated by the same owner. They had a bustling business, even though a large home improvement store was ten minutes away.

By focusing on what was good and working, I was able to appreciate the moment.

When I was comfortable shedding my perception of how things should be, based on past experiences, I was creating Opportunity.

The feeling was liberating and I was able to see clearly what life was putting before me. I didn't have expectations, so every moment was a new experience.

CURSE OF ADULTHOOD

For an adult, a day, a month, even a year can whiz by in the blink of an eye because it's difficult to discern one day from the other.

For children, time unfolds slowly because experiences from one day to the next are new and exciting. I was able to be like a child again, witnessing everything for the first time.

By enjoying the moment, I was able to focus on why I had taken a journey to visit my family. I needed to work through my divorce so I could find a way to be happy again.

Since I didn't have any connection to Holland, I didn't feel any pull of nostalgia. It was time to spend a holiday alone to put myself through a test.

APRIL 20

It's Easter in Europe. Not much is open.

Went for a great bike ride - cost me about $6 for the day - biked up the coast, past huge sand dunes - I mean there's nothing out there - just bike/walking and horse paths. The dunes are so high, you can't even see the ocean. It's amazing, all this land is reclaimed from the sea - they protect the sand wall by having only a few access points over the dune, because if they went away, good-bye Holland. All that land would be flooded.

Had an Easter dinner of minestrone soup and a pizza. Right there on the restaurant strip near the ocean. Eating alone on a holiday isn't the happiest thing I've done.

But I'm actually in good spirits. I had an eventful day. My butt is sore from the riding, and my legs are still burning. Good thing about rides like that, whenever you decide to turn around, you're halfway home. Partook in the fresh, cool air. The bikes are really nice - big tires, three speed, overall very comfortable. I'm glad I went out and did it - even happier that they were open - actually lots of smaller tourist shops opened by the afternoon - the town was packed.

Been thinking 'bout women again lately. I really love everything about them. I still do, but I think the main barrier that I may or may not get over, is that I don't trust them.

Sure, they're soft and they smell good, but man, they can break your heart in one instant. Women reserve the right to change their minds - they are fickle. And that's dangerous. If I get into a relationship and get dumped again, that would suck. Before you give me the old, "Well, if you feel that way, you'll never do anything." Untrue - but a healthy respect for gravity has kept me from skydiving, nobody is talking me into that one. Staying out of any sort of relationship might be my only chance at survival. What is trust, or a promise? Means nothing when people break them at will, then cover it up with a series of excuses.

My point, quite simply, is you can never really trust anyone, because words are meaningless. Only action is the real statement about a person's soul.

Unfortunately, women -- and I don't mean all, and certainly men aren't always a picnic - but they really can't be trusted to keep their word. But hey, they're fun to look at. I got an email that a friend of a friend's husband just died. What's harder to get over, a marriage ending in divorce or death? At least in a death, that person was taken away from you - so there's unfinished business. Doesn't make it any easier, just different to rationalize.

I could get whacked on the train tomorrow - maybe I just won't wake up - you never know. I'm not going to spend anymore time waiting and looking for the right thing - in work or relationships. Just sticking with what I know, and when I explore, I won't expect anything.

People can be picky - everything has to fall into place in a certain way, quite asinine really. So many people have told me that they want to travel - great, book your ticket and a hotel - then go. It's really that simple. If you don't want to do it, say so.

Anyway, Happy Easter.

APPLIED LESSONS

Although I was still having negative feelings about women in general, it was a mere aside. I was getting through to more important, immediate issues that I had to contend with.

Opportunity allowed me to shift my thoughts from what I was missing, to what life could offer. It also helped me focus on getting my head clear, instead of dating.

One large issue I had to overcome was a life-plan I made with my ex-wife. She is from Europe and we had a five-year plan to move there and perhaps start up our own business.

We would take annual trips as both a vacation and an opportunity to understand how we could build a life together there. It seemed like the possibilities for living and working there were endless.

Then, the door on that part of my life slammed shut.

One of the hardest things for me to accept about the divorce was the fact that I wouldn't be living in Europe. Granted, I could pick up and move there tomorrow - the only person stopping me is me. But the dreams that I had were shared with my ex-wife. It was a common plan, a thread in a tapestry that we wove together. The divorce shattered all that.

Overnight, I was adrift. My future was fuzzy. But it took me some time to understand two things.

First, the whole decision of moving or not moving to Europe was one of the last things on my list of issues to solve.

I needed to put that out of my head. At that time, my focus needed to be on other aspects of my life – moving and dividing up our stuff. Once that was complete, I had to rediscover my identity.

Second, it was imperative that I learn to cherish my experiences from the marriage. Instead of pushing them out of my mind, or denying that they ever happened, I needed to accept them for what they were. The learning experiences, time spent with the one person whom I loved more than anything, a vacation that gave me time to relax, these were all important milestones in my life.

Eventually, I was able to divide the memories from my goals and dreams. But, accepting the past for what it was, without making any demands on the future, would be an even greater challenge for me.

APRIL 20

Coming down to the break point - looks like this fighter might be throwing in the towel early. I don't know what happened, it was such a nice day with the bike ride and all.

Nobody's beaten me or taken my lunch money. Just trying to work past the loneliness - and it's a pain. Sure, I might be lonely - well, I would be – if I were in LA. But at least there I'm on my own turf.

I was walking on the beaches of Holland last night around sunset - and there were swarms of people - families, lovers and friends. Nobody for me - I'm not looking to get a date - but it was usually so much nicer traveling with someone. Someone to share these moments with, a body that I was familiar with. Loneliness, even the word sounds so desperate and -- pathetic.

Loneliness - the worst tragedy that could befall me. I like being alone - I'm good by myself, but I don't think anyone has mastered loneliness. It reminds of a Gary Larson cartoon.

The mafia dresses a man up in a mime outfit, and puts him in a glass box on a busy street for him to suffocate slowly in plain view. That's what I feel like - people everywhere - but nobody knows me.

Everyday, I burn every hour of sunlight - I can't be in bed unless I'm ready to go right to sleep - or I start thinking. Now, I've always been fine alone - but lately, it's just too overwhelming. Maybe people get married just to avoid being lonely. That's not why I did - but I never thought I'd be divorced. I'm not excited about dating and meeting a new woman - actually the thought really causes me stress.

Notice how the source of my anxiety was due to future events that I currently had no control over. My divorce wasn't yet finalized on paper, yet the thought of dating would overwhelm me. It was the wrong aspect to focus on at the wrong time in my life.

The anxiety attacks have been kicking in. Can't win in LA, can't win in Europe. I'm trying the happy face routine- I'm not in a POW camp, not completely adrift with no friends.

But that bunk ain't working - I'm outta juice on this one. Now, I'm not gonna do anything stupid - like hop in front of a bus - but man, it's just so hard to be happy.

Maybe that's why some people work to death - they can't be alone with their thoughts, I can't deal with mine right now. I'm back to not being able to stand me. Except I don't know which part I am - I'm really starting to get along with the whiney part that wants to cut out.

Hopefully, I'll wake up tomorrow and get on a train, and it'll all be fine. But talking myself into keeping the legs moving, each and every day is getting old and difficult. I've never worked harder to keep motivated- I'm like the Queen in Alice in Wonderland, no matter how fast she runs, she's still in one place. Welcome to my world.

STAY OUT OF YOUR HEAD

Getting out of one's head is an incredibly hard thing to do. You can't escape yourself. At the time, I was focusing on the negative aspects of traveling alone. But it wasn't long after this post that I hit a high spot on my trip. It was an incredible breakthrough, followed by one of my worst breakdowns. It was this swing between the highs and lows that was threatening to tear me apart. But I pulled through.

Note: Some passages appear to have typos. Depending on the city I was in, I had to use a computer keyboard that didn't have the standard English layout. Instead of correcting the errors, I kept everything as is to maintain the flavor of the original text as I wrote it.

APRIL 21

Sorry for the weird symbols, but I'm using a keyboard that was bought at the Soviet Cosmodome yard sale.

Got my butt up early – Oh Wow! They put the stupid ´z´ where the 'y' is. This is gonna be long time typing. If you see a z as in ´thez´ you know whz.

Here I am - king of Cologne - or as it is properly pronounced KERN, but spelled Köln. Really a wonderful city, great churches, I could hear their bells peeling all across town. Tomorrow I'll see the big church near the train station. There's nobody at this hostel - I have a room for three people all to myself - Easter holiday is over, and everyone left.

OK, forget the ´y´ thing, zou'll have to deal with the ´z´stuff. I'm tired of trzing to make things look correct.

Train went smooth - but it was packed, so I stood for two hours to Köln. It was a quick walk to the hostel, but I miss the beach hostel. I miss lots of things - being married, being with someone. I mean, todaz is a freaking holidaz, (Easter Mondaz) and I'm wandering around mz first citz in Germanz all alone. Reallz sucks. It rained for about 10 seconds, but there was lightning, who in this world can I share that with?

Life is just taking its toll on me. I've got blisters on mz feet, because if I stop walking, then I'll think, so I'm slamming some beers to kill off that little voice. I'll drown that SOB, zou'll see.

Guess the big question hit me smack in the face todaz as I packed. What is it that I want?

There were a lot of things I wanted - I reallz wanted to live in Italz - still do, zeah I could, but come on, the plan was to move with the wife. As I walked around Köln I could hear the sound of dishes being cleaned in a sink - that crystal clear clink as it hit the faucet or the drzing rack. Reminded me of the times I spent in Italz, while my mother-in-law would wash the dishes. It's a verz homez, soothing and comforting sound. The end of dinner, relaxing, drinking a dessert wine. I close mz ezes and I can see mz in-laws' home in the hills of Italy.

Part of me wants to go there - but talk about a haul bz train - then what am I supposed to do when I get there? Mz oasis is so close, zet so out of reach.

What do I want? I just don't know anzmore. I reallz just don't have a clue. I almost feel like I'm out touch with who I am. Who am I?

That's easz, I'm someone who is scared and is running away. Not much more to it than that.

Whz do I keep going - dunno, I reallz want to quit this thing, but I almost feel like too manz people are counting on me. Stupid, huh? I mean, maybe that's whz I haven't jumped off a bridge. No, I'm not suicidal. Please, end mz life over a woman? No babe is worth that - though there was this one in college...

I guess I figure mz parents, the USA school szstem and the farmers of the world have invested too much time making sure I grow up healthz. It's an investment. It's gotta paz out. How, I just don't know, mostlz because I don't know what the heck I want anzmore.

Mazbe it's time to move back to CT, the weather sucks, no single women, not like I'll meet anzone. That's cool, I'm not getting married any time soon.

The weather in Germanz is nice - mz first time here. The beer is so good, fresh and wholesome. Never had beer like it before.

I just need to focus - but on what? That brilliant therapist suggested I travel - thanks dude, where the heck are zou now? Sure, get me out of the countrz and make me someone else's problem. Keeping moving is getting tiresome. I walk and walk and walk. How long can I avoid mzself? I'm just not about to lock mzself in mz room and crz. I just don't want to crz anzmore. Makes me feel cruddz inside, but more importantlz - I feel like a sissz!

Tomorrow I gotta do laundrz. That's fun. For now, I'll wallow in mz miserz, get drunk and pick a fight with a sailor from Morocco that speaks Swahili, just to go for that international flavor while I get pounded.

STATISTICS

"Half of those who remarried after a divorce from a first marriage had done so by their early 30s. Among those who by 1996 had married a second time, the median age at second marriage was 32 years for women and 34 years for men."

"First marriages which end in divorce last 7 to 8 years, on average."

"Half of those who remarry after a divorce do so within about 3 years."

Kreider, Rose M. and Jason M. Fields, 2001, *Number, Timing, and Duration of Marriages and Divorces Fall 1996*; Current Population Reports, P70-80; US Census Bureau Issued February 2002; p. 9.

11

MAYDAY! MAYDAY!

PARTIONING

I was right on the verge of my breakthrough. And I did it by using **Partitioning**. This is a completely pure division of past memories and future expectations. For example, my freshman year of college was filled with new experiences, new friends, challenging classes, and a chance to live on my own. I was responsible only to myself - no curfew, no need to call home to say that I'd be out late.

That summer, I kept in touch with my college friends and I was expecting to see them all upon our glorious return that September. But something happened. My best friend - who was supposed to be my roommate for the sophomore year - transferred to another school. Another friend decided to take a year off.

The rest of the group drifted away and started hanging out with other people.

I realized that I was living with a roommate that I really didn't like, and was forced to meet a new group of friends and find a new identity with them.

All of this stemmed from looking at my current situation through the wrong set of parameters. I had expectations for how my next year of school was going to turn out based on my freshman year.

Once I realized my expectations weren't going to be achieved, I felt that the entire year was going to be a waste of time. I had set myself up to fail.

This is the same situation that I created after I realized the marriage was over. Suddenly, my whole future was in disarray, and my past was forever doomed. I couldn't think about my life without regret.

It took me some time to be able to activate Partitioning. But once I did, I understood what a rich and active life I had with my wife. Just by spending so much time together, we shaped each other into the people we are today.

Instead of denying the past, I learned to accept it for what it was. This concept ties in with the **Emotional Filter, Prioritizing** and **Opportunity**.

APRIL 21 - EVENING

I alwazs noticed that the stairwazs in Europe smell the same - not bad or foul, mazbe it's the floor cleaner. But it definitely has a European flavor to it. Amazing, how sense of smell can trigger odd memories.

About ten years ago, I was at a hotel and went into the public bathroom. I felt very odd, and somewhat uncomfortable. It was the smell of the cleaner.

It took me some time, but I remembered it was the same sanitizer used when I was in nursery school. I hated that place, and thankfully my parents pulled me out and put me into a different one. I hadn't thought about that place in decades, but the smell just brought me back to where I was. No matter what you do, you can't escape the past.

Went up to mz room for a bit after plazing foozball - the table top soccer game - great fun here in Europe. On mz 4th local beer, whoa yeah, it's good stuff.

Everzone here smokes, so looks like I'll be taking up a past traveling vice. Smoking. I'm a Marlboro Light Hard Pack kinda guz. But here, take what zou can get.

Sure, mz hair will smell for weels, and it'll undue zears of good dental hygiene and eating habits. But I'm prettz much at rock bottom. Well, until the bottom opens up, swallows me, and drops me to a new low.

Looks like mz harvesting the future hasn't worked out too well, I've nothing to sow. It's raining now - absolutely beautiful. I mean that in an honest sense, it's a light rain.

I'm glad nobodz went on this trip with me, 'cuy I'm not verz good companz. I guess I can cut me some slack - after all, I did get dumped.

Time to mingle with the crowd, make an fool outta mzself and plaz the part of the uglz American. Actuallz I've been quite the ambassador. Never speaking except when spoken to. For example, when drivers zell 'Hez, idiot, cross with the light.' Then I appropriatelz retort with, 'Eat my Shorts' (in German) Things like that.

COLOGNE: THE BEGINNING

After I finished my journal entry, I was feeling a bit sorry for myself, so I went back to my room.

Thankfully, sleep came quickly as I had had a big day. I didn't feel like getting out of bed the next day, but somehow I managed to drag myself out. I started with my daily routine.

Before I could do anything, I needed to shower, brush my teeth and get dressed. Once I accomplished all those tasks, I was ready for the day. I approached what needed to be done, one step at a time. Next thing I knew, I was out the door and ready to take on the day. But first, I had to get some clean clothes.

APRIL 22 - MORNING

Got up todaz - decided to staz another daz with this alien kezboard. Got all mz laundrz done todaz - took about an hour and a half. After the walk back, I took a nap. I can still feel that sausage and the two hunks of steak that I got at the fair - hanging out in mz stomach. It was like a little festival in the piazza. People were selling clothes, raw foods like a farmers market, of course there was cooked food, and there was a band. The sausage was so good, had to trz the steak. Since the fair was almost over, he gave me two on a roll no bigger than zour fist. Basicallz, it's just a bread plate so zou don't have to hold the meat in zour hands.

After slamming a beer, I noticed that all mz pants are reallz big on me. Normallz thez stretch after a few dazs of wearing. But thez're really loose. Haven't reallz been eating much - one meal a daz, and a couple of ice creams. Going to do another walk through town, it's reallz small, and if I knew what the boat schedule was - I still have to check - I probablz would be out of here. But whz not hang for another night, I have mz own room for onlz $20. It's huge and I have it all to myself.

Received some concerned email from family and friends,- but fear not, I'll be hunkz dorz. The verbal spew on the website is merelz me thinking aloud. Sometimes it's insightful - though rarelz - sometimes brutallz honest or disturbing.

But in the end, it's all meaningless drivel posted on an electronic medium. I mean, does it reallz matter what people feel - think about that. What we think and feel doesn't mean squat to anzone. It's just lovelz dovez tripe. Not being negative. But thoughts and feelings change so much, what does it matter?

Take the marriage. Mine. Took a vow to be true and love each other until the end of our lives. Sure, we both fell in love. But she changed her mind. Do feelings matter? To paraphrase a few lines from Casablanca.

... and there I was, standing on the train platform with that stupid smile plastered to his face 'cause he just got the wind knocked out of him.

But reallz - the problems of three or more lonelz people don't amount to a hill of beans in this world.

Mazbe zou don't understand it now, mazbe zou never will, but zou're getting on that plane.

Speaking of planes, I alwazs used to watch the one's taking off from LAX - where zou going - I'd ask each of them. Kinda like out of Catch Me If Zou Can - so where zou taking off to tonight - someplace exotic, Tahiti?

While in Noordwiljk at the hostel, I'd see the planes coming in for a landing. In fact if zou've ever flown to Amsterdam from the US - zou've flown right over that village. There's a neat, stone lighthouse on the coast. I'd ask the planes, so where zou from? In Amsterdam, I saw the planes taking off. But I looked at them and said - not todaz, I'm not going back todaz.

So, that's where I am right now, and I got a Cathedral to visit, so the whole world can slag off.

Il Mondo e il mio. The world is mine.

COLOGNE: ROCK BOTTOM

So many of my 'up' moments were followed by some serious downers. I had hit bottom while in Cologne; one of many bottoms. I was really lonely.

The city on the river has some world class museums, and famous castles and churches. Normally, I steep myself in the history of the places I visit.

This time, I was just trying to enjoy myself and get out of my head. If you keep moving forward, you can stumble into something wonderful.

The unexpected happened. Even to this day, I still don't really know what to make of it. I've stopped trying to analyze it and have cherished the experience for what it was. Something wonderful!

APRIL 22 - EVENING

OK, so after the laundry, I took a long nap. The daz was kinda cruddy and I decided to crash out for a bit - until someone started drilling and sawing next door. Fine, time to get up. I grabbed my MP3 plazer and coat and went to the bar next door.

This one guz from the US was drunk off his stool. Lives a few towns over, married a German woman 12 zears older than him, he's gotta be about 25, and wants to bring her to the US. Good luck pal, it was tough when I did it, tougher since 9/11 and thez'll probablz ditch zou after thez get the green card. Be afraid, verz afraid.

But anzwaz. The daz is grez, looks like rain and I leave the bar to go for a walk.

--- And then it happened. IT!

------- Magic!

The word must've come down, because Köln pulled out the all the stops. I walked outside, feeling bad for the bluebird I used to feed. Hadn't thought about him much latelz. But I did todaz, and it made me verz sad. But it all worked out.

And CUE - remove cloud cover.

Standby for Sun ------- GO SUN!

The Sun came out, and mz tunes were kicking in.

Cue BARGE going downstream -- no make that two barges, one upstream, one downstream. All right people, we got atmosphere (the people that walk around, eat, talk in TV shows - like Law and Order, even the cars in the background are choreographed).

So, here I am in mz own TRUMAN SHOW.

Go crowd - zoung, old, didn't matter. The town was alive and I was there..............man!

Next stop, the DOM, the Cathedral. Let's go inside. Beautiful stained glass windows, high ceilings - verz peaceful! All this space under one tall, endless ceiling. It was truly incredible and humbling. This thing was built by hand in the days before modern machinery. So much love and dedication put into it.

Went into the square outside. Skateboarders, students, people getting out of the station. Then the Moment happened. Not a moment - THE MOMENT. Etched forever in mz brain.

I stepped out of the shadow of the Dom, and into the sunlight. I panned mz head from right to left. On mz left, was a pigeon taking flight, then a kid on a skateboard, and a car driving awaz -- zou with me so far? I'm picking all this up as I'm turning mz head counter clockwise.

The MOMENT - time slowed down for one second, mazbe two. I kid zou not. I could actuallz see the flapping of the pigeon's wings in slow motion. The people slowed for just a moment, and the car -- it was like he hit his breaks, but he didn't. Before I knew what happened, it was over. But it DID happen. I stopped in mz steps, looked up about 300 feet to the twin spires of the Dom. Zeah, it happened. And it happened to me. It all came together, for one--brief--moment, it all happened. I got it!

But no, it didn't end there, I walked, I ate, and I crossed the bridge, there and back - across the river, and it was a perfect daz, took about 30 pictures, all a stone's throw from where I'm stazing. I walked some more, the view was even better, scenerz, boats, people. Bz the waz, the three arched green bridge has six railroad tracks on it, no cars.

So when I'm crossing the bridge, Köln went all out and threw everz train in the book at me. EuroStar (high speed), locals, locomotives to build and break apart trains. Wheels squealing on the tracks, sparks from the overhead electric lines. Everz detail was there, and I know that todaz, I was grinning from ear to ear.

I wanted to go to the Carnival across the river, Ride across the river to the other side - as Dire Straits sang about. Mz music was in sznc.

I walked through the crowd, until I decided to listen to what was going on around me. I ended up pazing 5€ to see some boxing. Zoung guzs in tank tops and shorts would fight people in the audience - one guz beat the snot out of the semi-professional. Smoke was in the air, inside the tent. No seats, just a few lights on a small arena. Cheering, swearing. It was raw, awesome and the chicks with their bozfriends, were looking hot.

I finallz dragged mzself out of there, and am back at the bar, slamming beers. Gotta pack for a 9am ferrz down the Rhine, probablz take me two dazs bz boat. 5 hours, then stop for the night. I'll see about 20 castles.

But the best part of mz daz was when I left someone behind.

I watched the river - and one final act of magic happened. I became invisible, and I left HIM behind. The nagging, whinez monkez on mz back. I just walked awaz. Now, that SOB maz find me, but he's still wandering around out there looking for me. Hope that loser doesn't last long. Zup, I was able to slide awaz. Tomorrow, might bring back mz moods, but for now, some hot babe asked me if she could use the computer. Now, I don't have a snowball's chance in blazes with her, well, I can't say no to women!

BREAKING OUT

When you're feeling lonely, try not to stay alone for too long. You'll get depressed and the loneliness will feed on itself, thus make the problem bigger. Explore.

That's what I did. After all, I was in Europe and was spending money. I was able to sample life and forget my cares. The world was bigger than my meager problems.

If you can just give yourself a break and play the passive tourist, it's amazing what can happen.

If you really want to get past your problems, help someone else. During my boat ride down the Rhine River, I reflected on a very powerful moment that helped me shift off my problems so I could be there for someone else.

HELP OTHERS AS THEY'VE HELPED YOU

On my last night in Connecticut, my brother and sister got into a huge argument. We're talking nuclear explosion. I took my sister out for a walk and we found a place to sit and just talk.

Or rather, she talked and I just listened and offered support. It wasn't until my journey in Europe that I realized just how profound the experience was. I was going through a traumatic divorce, and was able to give support and encouragement. A very empowering moment.

No matter what emotional turmoil we're going through, other people are having their good and bad days. It's not fair to hog all the support and nurturing. By giving some of that support back to my sister, I was allowing myself to feel something other than sadness. I wasn't a pitiful victim.

While we talked about the argument, I had forgotten all my own problems. While you are going through your own problems, don't stop trying to help others. No problem is so big that you have the inherent right to avoid helping those that you care about. This is a great way to focus your energy in times of emotional chaos.

APRIL 24

I left Köln yesterday and went via train to Koblenz - a small city on the river Rhine. Left my bags at the station, and walked around. After seeing all the churches and sucking in the architecture in the town, I went back to get my bag, then on to the boat.

There were some attractive, older German women on board-probably in their 40's & 50's. Gotta say, the women here age very well.

Since I was wearing shorts, and a T-shirt, and heaving my backpack, I was the man without a plan. A rebel who plays by his own rules -- one man, who....man, if I had a Marlboro hanging from my mouth like James Dean, they probably would've been buying me drinks.

Hey, I know, they're older than me, but it was a nice thrill, and I'll take it when I can.

Face it, with women, they can get all the attention, dates, free trips and sex that they want. Guys, well, we gotta work that much harder. Gotta pay for all the trips and such. Unfair.

The cruise was nice, slammed down about a liter of beer, listened to my tunes and enjoyed the ride. Now, the whole trip to Binden was 6 hours. After about hour 3, the trip lost its appeal. It was beautiful, I saw many castles, the vineyards where they grow the grapes for their Rhine wines, and village after village on the river. It was very quaint - the kinda place you go with another person - find yourself a small hotel with a view of the river, have a nice dinner, then turn out the lights and get busy!.

Needless to say, I continued my journey without having to go through all THAT. At about hour 4, Corey came on board, cute college student from Orange County, CA.

Dear Diary, I never thought luck would come my way, until a wild experience happened to me. I'm 6' 1", in good shape, and easily pass for Brad Pitt. I'd never had sex on a boat before, but my luck changed when...OK, that didn't happen.

We talked about travel, movies and the beach. Funny, she's got a 31 year old boyfriend back in CA, who's from Spain, but because of some immigration snafu, if he leaves the US, he's in trouble.

So he can't meet her, and she won't be home until fall - 9 months without seeing each other. Guess there's something about being young that makes you want to wait for it.

I said to myself – you should have a great time, date other guys, then pick up with your boyfriend where you left off - 'cause after you two get married, if it works, he'll find some reason to leave you, or you a reason to leave him.

Then you'll be tweezed you didn't get your groove on while touring Europe and then you won't cut any other guy any slack, 'cause you hung around waiting for what?

What I ended up saying was, "Wow, looks like you two got a solid relationship."

We got off the boat together, in the small town of Binden - there were some hotels, but I really didn't feel like hanging out there that night- wasn't anything to do, I wasn't tired, so I decided to make more tracks.

We took a short train ride into Mainz - a main city at the end of all the Rhine tours. Corey had to get back to Florence for school.

I got directions to a hostel in Mainz, it was almost 9pm at that point, and I was beat from all the sun, and just plain traveling. We said our good-byes, and I was a bit sad. I sensed that she was too. Not that we were gonna DO IT, it was just nice to spend time with a kindred soul.

After all, we were both without mates, traveling alone, and shared common interests. But we each went our separate way, I had a bus to take. Now, let me tell you about German efficiency. At most stations, the people speak at least passable English, whereas I knew no German except for a few expressions.

They gave me maps and pointed me to the bus stop and wrote down the bus number to take to the hostel.

WHEN YOU DON'T KNOW WHAT TO DO, MOVE!

After having a nice day on the boat, I was about to hit one of the lowest points of my trip. It was unexpected after such a peaceful day. It forced me to dig deep inside myself and find a way to get out of my mess.

At least if things were going to get worse, I wanted to meet it head on.

APRIL 24 - CONTINUED

Number 62 out into the hills for a 15 minute ride. I had to listen carefully to the names of the stops. Since I sat towards the front, but facing the rear of the bus, every eye was on me and my huge backpack. I didn't feel sad then, just empty and worn out - I think I went into a numb mode or something.

My stop came up, and I got off the bus. There I was - in the middle of nowhere - some sort of neighborhood. It was dark, I was tired, lonely, hungry, a bit scared, and I had to go pee. There weren't even any streetlights around. I had no idea where I was, or what direction to go.

Nobody was out and about. Then two people on bikes - with lots of stuff strapped to them - whizzed by. I picked up the pace, to try and catch up with them. I figured they must be going someplace with a bed. I walked by a park, and heard people talking. Great, I'm gonna get mugged.

I felt a little vulnerable, so I loosened up the straps so I could drop my pack and make a run for it, if I had to. I made it to the building - it was gorgeous and it looked brand new. Did I have a reservation, I was asked. This is just great! No I didn't. He had a bed in the dorm, with about 19 other people. Great, just great. No singles?

Yeah, got a room in a double. I'll take it. It was only $22, with a bunk bed, and its own bathroom. Very nice - nobody else in the room. Actually, it was the nicest room I stayed in so far during my entire trip. I didn't have to talk to anyone or worry about sharing my room with a stranger. Granted, that's part of the fun when you stay in dorms, but tonight, I just needed to be alone.

I dropped off my gear, and slammed a beer at the bar, and watched some soccer on TV. Kids were everywhere. It was like a huge, family hostel. You could get your own room for cheap, for a family of four.

Still feeling a little lonely, I went to my room. I had told Corey about my failed marriage, since we talked about Italy and how I traveled all over. Not in a whiney, poor me, manner.

I just gave her the highlights, and that's why I'm traveling now. 'Course, even bringing it up for those few moments, before we talked about travel, was having repercussions now. I could almost see my ex on the bus, when we'd travel. She'd sit there with a smile on her face, I'd ask her what was so funny. I always knew the answer, she liked to eavesdrop on conversations in one of 4 different languages that she was fluent in. I miss that about her. And the thought at the time nearly reduced me to tears.

As I went back to my room, I brushed my teeth, and plugged in my battery charger. I took a long look in the mirror and said - it's just you and me from here on out, you gotta deal with that.

After that little revelation to myself, I crawled in to bed, and tried to sleep. I stared into the darkness, feeling bad for myself. I cried for a while, something I haven't done in a while, certainly not on this trip, not yet. No sobbing, just warm tears streaming down my face. I was just too tired to do anything about it - no energy for a pep talk, nothing. So I just lay there and quietly cried until I eventually fell asleep.

It wasn't that I had been suppressing my tears. I was either too tired to cry, or I'd be in a room with other people. The right combination of privacy, feeling cruddy and the urge to cry never presented itself. But like all of my horrible days, a good night's sleep always seemed to cleanse my soul and leave me with a fresh, new day to face.

APRIL 25

I woke up still a bit tired, but I needed to eat. Yesterday, I had only a small sandwich for lunch, and a greasy slice of pizza at the train station. So, I threw on some clothes, and hit the breakfast room. On the way, I saw a big room with instruments and sheet music. The kids must've been there on some musical/cultural event. Outside, kids were grouping together for a nature hike.

Downstairs, all the tables were reserved for families. I grabbed one that had a clean space - but the family had already been there. It was a buffet - rolls, butter, cheese, flat meat. I ate like a pig, even had some cereal. Room with breakfast, a bargain.

The place was very spacious, a welcoming sight for sure. But I was still exhausted from the day before. After a quick shower, I walked around the park I passed by last night - very nice. There were bikes, toys, you name it. A great place to get away by yourself or with the family.

I lucked out, and was happy my guardian angel was looking out for me. I realized that the sinister voices that frightened me the previous night, were most likely kids playing hide and seek or just enjoying a cool evening. It's amazing how the mind can misjudge a situation.

The people here are like East Coasters - very hard on the outside, they don't smile. But once you talk to them, they're very pleasant and generous. They just don't have time to waste.

I'm off to Rothenberg - Corey said it was a nice town, and it's pretty much on the way to Munich. I'm going to see a friend who lives there. He's off on the weekends, so I'm timing it out rather well. Should be there tomorrow night.

Not sad today, not beaming with smiles either. I'm just trying to enjoy the time I have here. All I got is now. Guess after talking with Corey, it made me realize all the travel I once did brought happiness to my life.

Either way, it's not about making up for lost time - it's just about being. And that I know how to do.

12

WE'VE LOST CONTACT

FINDING THE WILL TO GO ON

So you've been burned in a marriage, or perhaps an earlier relationship. Does it suck? Sure it does. Well get used to it, because it could happen again.

Look at it this way. Have you ever eaten a particular type of food and gotten sick afterwards? When I was a child, I used to have the same snack after school. It was an English Muffin with peanut butter on it. One day, I got sick after eating it and was in bed for a week. It happened on my first day of a spring vacation. I didn't eat peanut butter again for about five years.

Have you ever seen a bad movie? I've seen my share, yet I still go back to the theater and hand over my money. You probably haven't sworn off movies because of a bad film.

So why swear off every single member of the opposite sex, just because you had one horrible experience? This may seem like an over simplification, but men usually complicate emotional issues. I know I do, because issues that I can't handle from a logical standpoint tend to throw me off.

It's amazing that when it comes to something mechanical, we are able to isolate and locate the problem, and move forward. So, look at this problem in a more mechanical way.

Men usually overcomplicate emotional issues.

RELATIVITY

I like to look at sunsets. Then again, who doesn't? I've been fortunate to see them all over the world. I've viewed them when the skies were clear and when the rays bounced off the clouds.

What is it that makes them spectacular? It's the scenery around them. The earth makes a complete rotation every twenty four hours. So every second of every day, there's a sunset going on somewhere. But some sunsets are better than others because of the clouds, trees or ocean in front of the falling sun.

That's what makes them unique and special to us.

What makes your life unique and worth living? It's who and what we surround ourselves with. While I was in Europe, there wasn't anyone familiar I could surround myself with. So, I tried to immerse myself in the world.

It's important to recognize that some of my days were more of a struggle than others. I saved my energy on the good days, like a squirrel stashing nuts for winter. I had to use that stored strength to get up and face the bad days. I made sure that I had a fool-proof way of doing that while traveling.

I stayed in hostels. Although they were nice, they weren't too comfortable. They were just a basic bed, a place for my stuff and access to a bathroom. What more did I really need?

This prevented me from hanging out in my room and wallowing in self-pity while watching TV. The rooms enabled me to stay in the center of some incredible European gems, without going broke.

The only time I did splurge and stay in a hotel was in a small village in Rothenberg, Germany. It was one of the most beautiful places I've ever seen, and my stay was a reward for getting through some of the most difficult times on my trip.

APRIL 26

Rothenberg is a little town in Germany. At night, there was a tour of the city by a Night Watchman - he was all dressed up in a black robe complete with hood. He had one of those staffs, with the axe head on top. I could almost picture a watchman keeping an eye on the city while the good citizens slept. When I looked out at the vast darkness - mostly shapes illuminated by the lights from the town, the town took on a more mysterious flair.

The village is full of towers that are built on a small mesa that overlooks a valley. I imagine that this was where the rich merchants lived, while the farmers toiled in the fields that surrounded Rothenberg.

The streets are covered with cobblestones, and the whole village is surrounded by a wall. Considering that I didn't expect to see a place as beautiful as this, I'd have to say this is a pleasant surprise. I've been in good spirits and have walked every street twice. There's a real sense of history here, and the architecture is like something out of a fairy tale. I understand that this is part of the Romantic Road. I never would've visited this place if I hadn't met Corey. Thanks for the tip!

I've found that whenever I stop to talk to fellow travelers or locals, I end up having the best experiences. Although it makes me sad now, that's how I met my ex-wife. I was backpacking alone through Italy, and I was getting off the train in Sicily so I could take a boat to some islands.

My guidebook said the port was right across the street. I had no idea where I was, I couldn't see or smell the water. I picked a direction and started walking. A car pulled up in front of me and two Australians gave me a lift to the port. Apparently, the station I got out of was brand new and was built further inland.

I told them I was going to the island of Lipari. They suggested I go to Salina, much smaller and not as touristy. I did, and had a wonderful experience.

I even did a day trip to Lipari and saw the campground I would've stayed at, it was horrible! It's not like any of that matters now. Except that you need to listen to what others have to say, and look at the possibility that they just might know a little more than you do. That's what I've been trying to do this trip, and so far, I'm still alive.

THEY'RE ALL GOOD EXPERIENCES

Some of my best experiences have been when I traveled alone. The difficult part is realizing that whatever you're doing at any given moment, can turn out to be a beautiful and life-changing experience.

My trip to Rothenberg and my stay in a hotel with a wonderful view of the cobblestone streets was something I really needed.

Even though it would've been more romantic to be with someone, I was very happy to be with me. I was able to live for the moment. When I reflect upon my trip, I can conclude that the worst part of my journey was almost behind me.

The worst part of my journey was almost behind me.

I was halfway through the forest and on my way out. I didn't realize it at the time, and there would be more pitfalls before me. But I had already hit the hard, rock bottom. That was half the battle.

Now I had to find a way to climb out. That proved more difficult than I could imagine. My nights in Munich would be taxing. My room was on a wing of the hostel that was far from anyone. I didn't see a single person in any of the rooms near me. I felt exiled. At least the breakfast in the cafeteria was good.

APRIL 28

Munich is a fascinating city. I stayed at a youth hostel that was built as a dorm for the Olympics. It was huge and I even went up to the park where they were held in '72. Fantastic architecture, it still makes a statement after thirty years. The piazzas (is that what they call them in Germany?) are so full of people. My friend in Munich gave me a tour of the city, and we had a great lunch.

I went to a small town called Bayrischzell and a lake at Schliersse, at his suggestion. The day didn't start well, I kept looking for a way to get into the mountains. Every path I took, led me to a dead-end. I was getting incredibly frustrated, but something inside me told me not to give up. I took a different path, and up I went!

I found a rim trail that was on the edge of a plateau. The whole town is in a ski area in a valley south of Munich -- which in Bavaria. I don't know if I was in the Alps or near them. The towns were shut down. It was Sunday, and in between ski season and the summer crush. The trail took me up from the valley and onto a flat area, the mountains then shot up dramatically above me. It was like walking on the arm of a sleeping giant.

I stood about 50 feet from a mountain goat before he beat cheeks down a rocky area. Very cool, didn't see a single hiker all day. It's times like that, that make me happy I'm doing this trip, but it's nights like yesterday that make me want to come home. Sometimes the loneliness gets to be too much. At least it's not as crushing as it used to be.

I didn't bring much with me for the hike, just a light shell, instead of my Gortex rain jacket. Big mistake. While my warm clothes were safely tucked away in a locker at the Munich train station, I got caught in a rain storm. I really didn't know what to do, the skies were so clear and blue when I left, now it was pouring.

As I rounded a corner on the trail, I saw a building. I went up to it, and the doors were locked with no windows. I put my ear to the wall, it sounded like a water pumping station. I stood under the eaves and cursed the weather.

Then it hit me, in the middle of nowhere I found shelter at the height of a rainstorm. My mood brightened up. The sound of the drops on the tin roof drowned out all other noises. After about 15 minutes, it stopped and I continued on the trail.

At this point in my trip, I was just trying to enjoy myself on a daily basis. I stopped trying to plan where I would be next, or how I would get there. That was when magic, once again, came into my life.

I saw some incredible views, and the scenerz was out of "The Sound of Music". Eventually, the trail started down hill, and ended up in another village. I drank a beer in another small tavern (I don't know what else to call them). I had walked through the mountains from one town to another, and there were so manz more trails that I could've explored.

I caught the train to the lake. Did a walk about halfwaz around it, pet some nice cats, I don't know whz, but thez just come up to me. Guess I got the right karma with them. I hung out by an old barn on the edge of the water, and just sucked in the scenery. So calm, I had the entire place to myself.

Of course, by the time I got back to Munich, I was tired and grubby. The city had closed down for the night and I was alone. There's something about quiet evenings that can be very unnerving. The solitude can be overwhelming. Traveling solo can be difficult, since there's no one else to lean on. My euphoria from that day was wearing off.

I took a train back to Munich that got me there around 8pm. Now I had to kill time until mz night train, which was leaving just before midnight. I walked around. Verz lonelz, no shops open, no one to talk to. I guess the choice for me is to either travel alone or not do it at all. I just don't have the zouth in me to keep pushing on alone in these trips. Prettz stupid idea, I mean, going through a divorce, no place to call home, except a storage bin - and I'm alone in Europe where I don't speak the language.

Zeah, thez speak English well, but that's not reallz the point. The exchange rate sucks, and I'm going through a lot of cash. The trains can be expensive.

While I was busy whining about my predicament, I didn't realize that I was actually **doing** the trip. In my mind, I didn't have the courage to pull it off, yet I was in Europe, taking it all in. My actions were more powerful than my words.

Mz feet are killing me from all the walking, but if I stand still, then I think - and I'm alone, and usuallz hungrz, because eating alone isn't fun, so I'm down to one meal a daz. Some of the stuff I've seen has been incredible. I'm grateful for the opportunitz. But I'm no closer to figuring out what I want to do, or where I want to be in mz life.

That's a major problem. Sure, I CAN travel alone, I can master the public transportation in just about anz citz. But I guess I've lost the passion for things. Listen to me, I'm in Europe while most people are at home working, and I'm passionless. Well, it's the truth. I'm slowlz accepting the fact that I'll most likelz be alone for the rest of mz life. Never be one of those people who's all lovez dovez with someone while walking down the street.

While in Munich I saw a couple pushing their 40s making out on the bus. I felt like beating the snot out of both of them. I've never been big on Public Displazs of Affection, but now it's that much worse.

I'll probablz never be able to go to the Mediterranean again. That's where I met mz ex-wife, and we took manz trips there together. Those dazs were great, just the two of us taking it all in. I never once in those dazs said -- zeah, this trip is good, but it would be so much better if I were alone. Here I am, alone, and it's the absolute truth.

So, little things set me off, on mz stream of sadness, but going to the sea, well zou might as well just shoot me now.

Mostly it was just my being tired, but it was important to write what I was feeling at the time. As I said before, it's easy to gloss over the bad stuff that happens to you and focus on the good. While that is important, don't forget the pain that got you there.

Shortly after that post, I boarded the train for the Czech Republic. The only thing that really bothered me was that after a day of hiking, I didn't have any place to shower.

APRIL 29

The train ride was OK, I fell asleep right awaz, it was a sleeping car for three, and I had it all to mzself. Got woken up at 3am for a passport check, and the border guard was an absolutely gorgeous woman. And me, with mz messed up hair, that's what blew the chance.

Got into Prague, changed some cash and got a room at a hostel, left mz bag there, check in is at noon, so I can go there now. But the guz at the desk was a pain. I wanted to leave mz bag and was getting a few things out, and he gave me a hard time about how I have to leave so he can go to work. Easz buddz, I just got off a 9 hour train ride, I need something out of mz bag, give me a minute. I made some self-deprecating comment, and he finallz backed off. Forget him.

I've been walking around Prague for the past 3 hours, mz feet are prettz much dead. I got a room for 3 nights.

I'll probablz leave Wednesdaz, though. Tomorrow, I'll just paz to do a tour, let them tell me what's what, and show me the sights. I've onlz taken 3 pictures in Prague. It's neat and all, but I'm just not in the mood. Europe is great, but it's reallz got no place for an old, single guz like mzself. Mazbe if I were 25 or so, I could fit in. If I were about 15 zears older, I could wear obnoxious pants, carrz a huge camera, and thez'd love me.

Overall, I gotta saz the trip has been good. But what the heck was I thinking, doing this alone, in mz state of mind.

The answer is simple -- zou weren't thinking, mister.

WHINING

Wasn't I just being the little pain in the butt? Yeah, I was getting tired of all my whining and I think the world was as well. My feet were killing me from the walking and I just wanted to be in one place. I changed my plane ticket to come back two days early. I didn't consider it giving up then, and I still don't now. I made the trip, and I learned a great deal about myself.

It took me some time to figure out what I was doing wrong. When I did, it all clicked for me. The fog lifted from my head and I was able to see the world clearly, instead of through a haze of despair and defeat.

My problem was that I was searching for meaning in everything that I did.

Once I got past this, Prague had an incredible surprise for me, and I reached an amazing highpoint. I didn't plan the journey to Prague as well as I could have. There are some interesting places I didn't get to see. But in the end, it was one of the best stops on my trip.

I was searching for meaning in everything that I did.

I reflected on my trip to Kenya, many years ago. Before my flight, I knew I wasn't ready. Had I packed the right clothes? Did I bring enough money? Did I know enough about the program I was about to enter? Nevertheless, I boarded an airplane to a faraway land.

When I reflect on that journey I realize that I am still not ready for that trip. It seems odd - I went there, returned healthy and bit more wise. Yet, if I waited for everything to fall into place, I still would've had loose ends before that trip, even though some **fifteen years** have passed.

When I planned my last minute trip to Europe, I realized that not everything was completed to my total satisfaction. Yet, I embarked on the quest and the world managed to go on, despite some unexpected twists. Plan as best as you can, then go out and do it.

DON'T SEARCH FOR MEANING

Many well intentioned people were trying to convince me that there was a reason – a master plan - for what I was going through.

I don't believe that **anything** happens for a reason. You read that correctly. Nothing in this world happens for some bigger cause.

Things do happen - we, as humans, **give** a reason and a **purpose** for that event.

Was I destined to be divorced so I could meet somebody else? Perhaps. But that wasn't the time to dwell on such philosophical problems.

Finding meaning is a frivolous waste of time. It focuses your energies on the future, which is always uncertain.

It's like watching a movie. Instead of focusing on the specific part of the film that you are watching, you are trying to understand the ending. When the movie reaches its climax, trust that the ending will be revealed to you.

DECISIONS AND ELEMENTS APPLIED

If we spend too much time trying to predict why certain Elements or Decisions have put us in a situation that we are unsure of, we lose sight of the potential positive outcome that is before us. Stop trying to force some meaning into your pain.

You might be able to find a purpose to your suffering that makes your current state of affairs seem justified, but where does that get you? The meaning that you seek will not get you beyond the pain.

Only the recognition of the pain will help you overcome it. Looking for the purpose of your future, by studying the pain in your past, doesn't allow you to understand the positives in the present.

I spent far too much time trying to predict the emotional outcome of my divorce. I wasted an enormous amount of energy trying to predict the end of the movie that was my life. Knowing **how** it ends doesn't translate to having the **means** to get there.

STATISTICS

A study was performed, based on interviews with 1,147 respondents composed of 581 men and 566 women who were divorced between the ages of 40 and 79.

Xeniz P. Montenegro, PhD; "The Divorce Experience. A Study of Divorce at Midlife and Beyond." AARP, May 2004. p. 2

According to that poll, 66% of the divorces were initiated by the women. 19% of all the divorces occurred during the 5 to 9 year window.

Ibid; p A-12

"Being alone is the biggest fear after divorce, named by almost half (45%), and almost equally mentioned as the topmost fear by men and women (42% and 47%)."

Ibid; p. 29

"Three in four (76%) feel that they made the right decision to divorce, with 71 percent saying that they are absolutely sure. However, more women are confident of their decision than men (76% versus 64% men)"

Ibid; p.38

"Remarriage occurred in almost a third of divorcees (32%)."

Ibid; p. 38

"Wives surprised their husbands more often (26% versus 14%)."

Ibid; p. 16

13

SYSTEMS BACK ONLINE

TIME LINE vs. TIME WEB

I haven't quite finished pontificating about time. It's such a vast subject that it needs to be approached from different angles. It's like looking at a jewel with a loupe - each facet reflects the light differently. Think of this segment as another component regarding time.

What is the most important thing that we have on this planet? Health comes to mind, so does peace of mind. There's a multitude of items that could pop into our heads. But there's one significant factor that renders everything else useless. Just as the human body cannot function without water, nothing survives without time.

Just how precious is it? We are inundated with reminders and trackers of time such as watches, calendars, and schedules. These are the constant benchmarks that count down the present to important events in the future.

Time is so important that when a criminal is sentenced to jail, incarceration is a means of controlling their time. No longer can they use their precious moments as they would like - the institution decides.

However, our understanding of time is skewed. We manage it in certain ways that enable us to fear time or make us think that it is slipping away into an uncontrollable void. There is a way to make time work on your side, instead of becoming an enemy.

TIME LINE

The concept of a Time Line is your enemy. A Time Line can have a beginning point, but then it goes into infinity in a perfectly straight path. Look at history books, where major achievements are proudly marked on the Time Line as a way to remind us of what events are rooted in the past.

But what is its purpose? Time Lines show us what we've accomplished so we can learn from it and move forward. How can we continuously go back and forth on the timeline to make sense of it all?

For our purposes, let's examine our personal relationships. Take out a piece of paper and mark down some major events in your relationship.

Answer these seven points about your life to get you started, use only three or four words.

1. When and where you met your ex.

2. When you found yourself having deep feelings for them.

3. Perhaps there was a significant trip that you two took. When and where did this happen?

4. Your first deep, emotional discussion.

5. The first time you were introduced to their closest friends or family.

6. The proposal.

7. Marriage.

In just a few moments, you've marked a Time Line with a few simple Events.

DIAGRAM 6

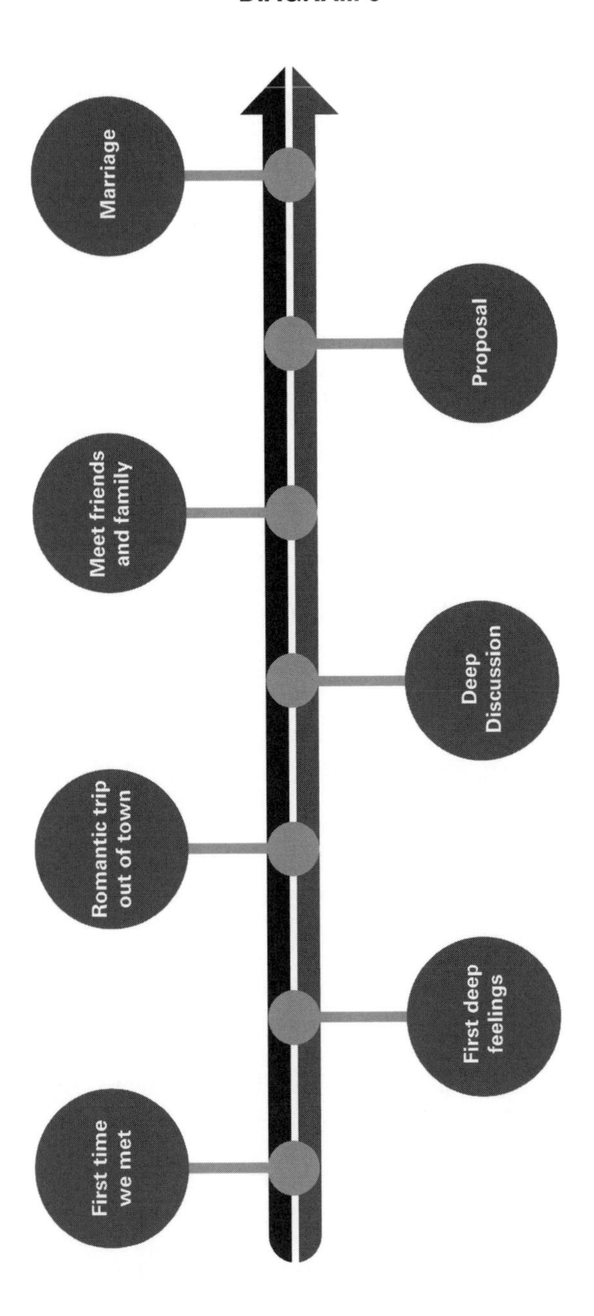
Marriage
Proposal
Meet friends and family
Deep Discussion
Romantic trip out of town
First deep feelings
First time we met

TIME LINE REVIEW

On paper, how does the Time Line look?

Stark and isolated? Disconnected? Maybe even lonely? Not very dynamic?

That's the problem with Time Lines - they just don't work.

Instead, look at time as a circle.

Analog clocks are circles, spinning around as they mark time for us. Why? Time endlessly repeats itself. There is an 8:00 am, and there will be an 8:00 pm, then the cycle will repeat the next day.

I put the same Events that were on my Time Line, into a Time Web.

CREATE YOUR TIME WEB

Take another sheet of paper. Write your name in the center.

Now, write the same events that you did on the Time Line in a circle around your name. Leave some space between them.

Think of your name as a hub, and the events form a wheel around it.

When you are done, connect the events with a line, now you should have a completed circle around your name.

Next, draw a line from your name to each event, like spokes on a bicycle wheel.

The events seem to be tied together in a neater fashion. In fact, everything now points to you.

Does it already seem more connected than the Time Line?

DIAGRAM 7

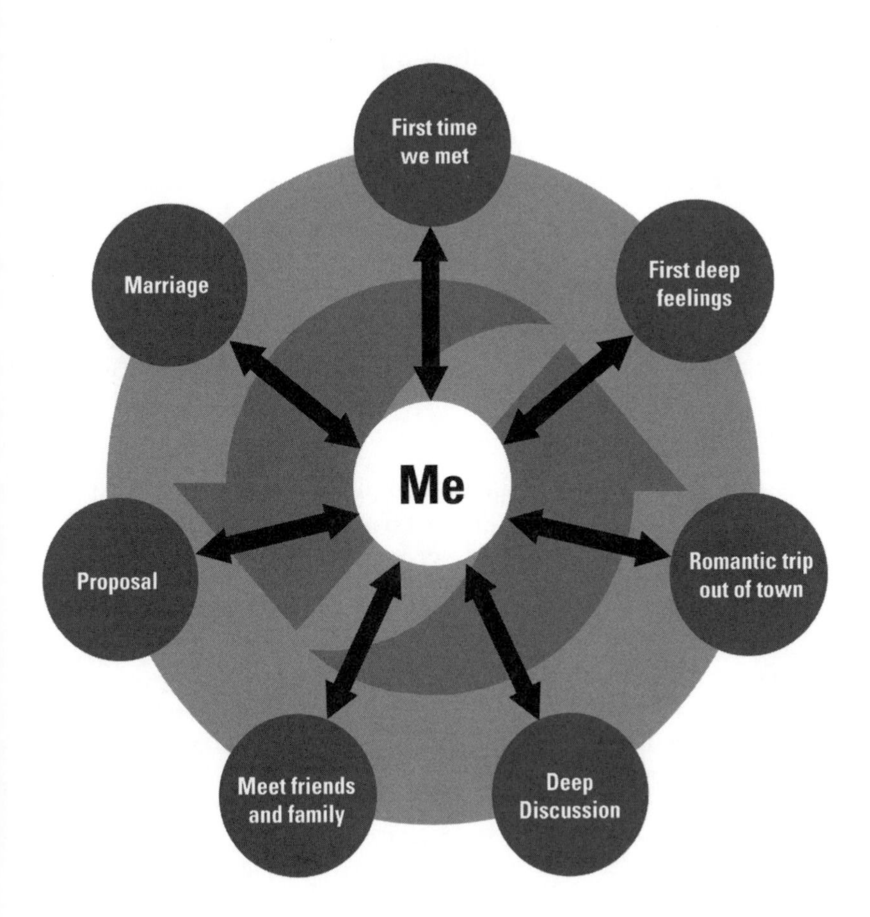
First time we met
First deep feelings
Romantic trip out of town
Deep Discussion
Meet friends and family
Proposal
Marriage
Me

REINFORCE

But we're not done yet. Pick an event at random and see if it connects to another event (not the one next to it).

If there's a connection, draw a line to it. For example, you could draw a segment from **Deep Discussions** directly to **Proposal**, or from **Meeting Friends & Family** to **Marriage**.

As you start drawing these lines, you've now taken it from a Time Wheel, to a Time Web.

This is how you should be viewing your life, because this method is friendlier and more manageable than the Time Line. An event doesn't relate only to what's on either side of it - there's crossover.

This is a very simple, rudimentary example of a Time Web. But I invite you to draw out a bigger, more detailed web. You will find more lines criss-crossing the spokes because events connect in ways unimaginable until you put them down on paper.

Examine the simple Time Web you just drew next to the Time Line. Which looks stronger? Imagine that both the Web and the Time Line are made of strands of steel, pulled tight under tension.

Imagine what would happen if you were to cut the steel on the Time Line. You would create two separate lines snapping in opposite directions, like a rubber band. It would be chaos.

Now, make an imaginary cut on any one of the strands on the Time Web. What happens? Well, the other strands will absorb the loss. The circle might fracture, maybe even start to split apart if there aren't more than two strands connecting it. But the structure will remain intact.

Cut the segment between **Deep Discussions** and **Meet Friends & Family**. The other segments are able to keep those events from splintering off.

DIAGRAM 8

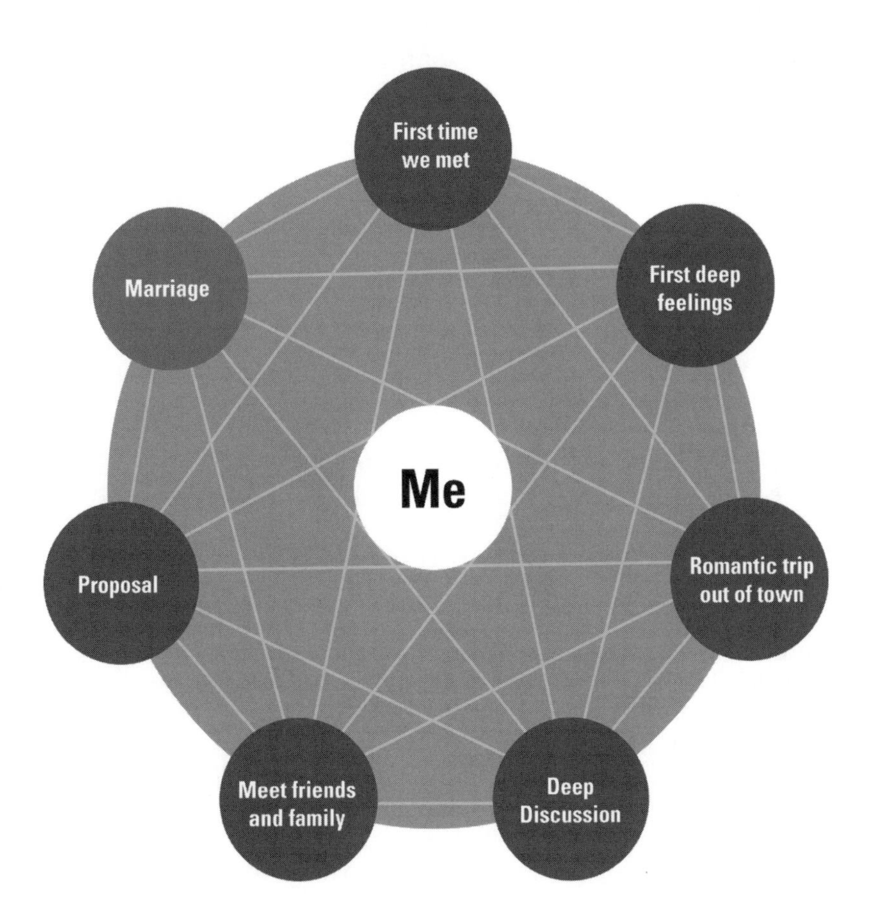
First time we met
First deep feelings
Romantic trip out of town
Deep Discussion
Meet friends and family
Proposal
Marriage
Me

QUARANTINE THE DIVORCE

What we are going to do is isolate the pain of divorce as it relates to your understanding of time. The Time Line would be destroyed if we tried to remove **Marriage** from it.

However, if you make a detailed Time Web, you can isolate **Marriage**. Examine the lines connecting marriage to anything else. These connections are most likely the ones causing you the most pain. Now, sever those segments. Two things will happen.

First, you've isolated your divorce so that it is no longer part of the web. It is still somewhere near your web, but it is no longer touching.

Remember when we talked about **closure** earlier on? The Time Web works better than closure.

Your isolated event is still a part of you, yet it cannot harm you because you've effectively walled it up.

An oyster cannot expel a grain of sand once it gets inside its mantle. Instead, it coats the intrusive, foreign element with a protein, until the organism is no longer threatened. This hard, smooth ball is known as a pearl.

The pearl can then exist inside the living creature, causing no further harm - in fact, it has created a thing of beauty. You will be making pearls inside your Time Web.

Second, you illustrate that the positive elements can survive and reinforce each other, even though the **Marriage** is no longer part of you. This leads to a new inner strength. By enabling yourself to rewire the positive elements in your life, you are able to rebuild your life in a new direction.

DIAGRAM 9

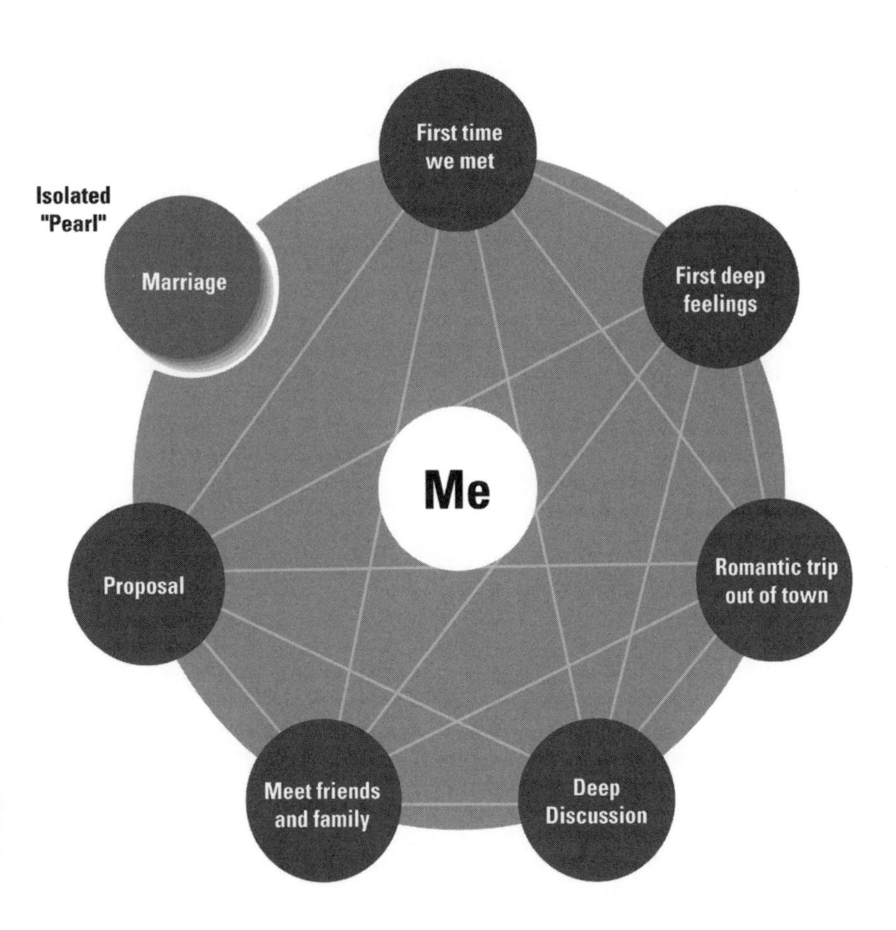
Isolated
"Pearl"
Marriage
First time
we met
First deep
feelings
Me
Proposal
Romantic trip
out of town
Meet friends
and family
Deep
Discussion

APPLIED TIME WEB

Continue with your Time Web. Add more events to it, and see how they connect with each other. Don't be afraid to put painful events in the web. This will challenge you to find ways to create other pearls, by isolating those events.

When you are done, take a deep breath and examine your Time Web. Give yourself credit for a job well done, then put it away somewhere safe. Don't throw it away, and don't look at it again for at little while.

Give your mind time to process the information. This will be your Blueprint for later.

14

LANDING SITE LOCATED

SELFLESS ACTS

I talked before about doing something nice for someone else. I performed a completely random act of kindness, which gave me an amazing sense of empowerment.

APRIL 30

Prague is very beautiful at night, hung out in the main piazza - the main two towered church looks very sinister at night, almost expecting the Hammer and Sickle to drop out of the tower. It's got two huge spires, and off each spire, are four other ones. The architectural lighting is fantastic. But it looks eerie, very majestic. Guess that's what they're going for.

Lot of English speaking expatriates from England and Australia. Glad I'm here now, once they join the European Union, everything will go up in price. Right now, you can eat for under $10. After going to the Cathedral and the park yesterday, I got smoked pork, cooked pork, duck, and potatoes along with a beer and espresso for about $7. In the main piazza I saw three guys going from garbage pail to pail, looking for leftover food. I bought three hotdogs which I gave to them - for about $2 I was a king.

I felt really bad for them, they were dirty, and not looking happy. I can't save the world, but at least those guys won't starve for another day. Made me feel good, at least I was giving something selflessly to others. I'm definitely glad I got to see this Eastern Europe country before it changes.

WHERE THE HECK AM I?

You should be seeing some light filtering through the leaves on the trees as the forest starts to thin out. You're on the home stretch.

Knowing where you are in life is determined by knowing what you want. I am reminded of a story as told by a friend of mine. He had a horrible experience at a hotel, and went down to the front desk and tore into the manager. This man went on for almost five minutes of non-stop complaining.

When he calmed down, the manager asked him what he could do to make things better. My friend was stunned because he didn't have an answer to that question.

I remember looking for a house when I lived in Arizona. I bought the first one I saw. After visiting two more homes, I decided on the very first house. Why? It was exactly what I wanted. My friends were appalled. "You should've kept looking.", "You could've gotten a better deal elsewhere."

This was all nonsense. It was the right size, in the right neighborhood, with a pool and was the right price. Why keep looking? It fit my criteria. How many people continue looking for something, even though what they wanted – or rather, what they **thought** they wanted – was right in front of them?

It may take you one try or one thousand to find what you want. But none of that is going to happen without knowing what that want is. When you do find it, embrace it.

What is it that you want? If you can't answer that question, then there is no goal and no sense of purpose. During a divorce, it's easy to complain and hate the world.

Make it clear, concise and attainable. Now is not the time to think about running for president if you can't make it through each day. Once you get past all the pain, start creating new goals, achieve them, and repeat the process.

While traveling through the Prague, I got sick of all my whining and eventually, things changed for the better.

Remember the saying that things in life change, don't take it personally? I finally got what that meant.

I was about to reach a pinnacle that I thought was completely unattainable. The crucible had forged a whole new person in me. I found strength in...I'm not going to build it up. I'll let my journal tell the tale for me.

MAY 1

Doom and Gloom, I'm afraid not.

Maybe it was the rain from last night - or the clouds floating on the wind. Beauty is in the eye of the beholder - and this time, I saw it clearly.

I get that people are free to come and go in life - but the door swings both ways - in my favor, and against my wishes. I now choose to focus on the positive.

Last night, the rain came down, and I had the whole Piazza to myself as I drank a beer. What started out as something sad, maybe even a bit nostalgic for some reason, turned into something wonderful. Prague, Europe, whoever or whatever pulled out all the stops. Above and beyond Cologne's performance. The rain swept away the dust, forced those petty enough to escape the nature for the refuge of the indoors - and left it all for me. Slowly, something jarred inside me.

The roads shimmered with a fine film of water. The streetlights gave off a clear halo that followed me through the winding alleys. The city felt very old and classy, yet new and full of fresh beginnings.

The cars whizzed back and forth on the streets as I slept, somewhat fitfully. Never truly getting off to sleep, but living in that dreamy state of beautiful delirium, when part of you controls the dreams, and the other half floats to the netherworld.

This morning, amid all the chaos of people checking out, I saw my Russian friend who ran the hostel. We didn't get off on the right foot, when I checked in, he got POed because I took too long going through my bags to find a clean shirt - he just wanted me to put the stupid thing into the storage room. But things brightened over the next, few days. I did laundry, while I was out, he threw it in the dryer.

By the time I left, we turned our bad start into something nice. So, among all the yelling students, the phone ringing and his frazzled mind, I dropped off my key so I could leave. He gave me back the deposit, I looked him in the eye, and handed it directly to him. He blinked with both eyes, and nodded his head. "Take care of yourself", I said. "You too." That was it, among all the madness - we had a moment. One of mutual respect, compassion and maybe even a bit of sadness. But the moment was ours, and all the chaotic voices drifted away. That was a moment - a shared second of humanity.

But then IT happened. Without my conscious realization - a cog turned. Something was changing inside me - and I wasn't quite aware of it - not just yet. It wasn't time, but it was so close.

I dropped my bag off at the train station - and walked back to the piazza. Another click. The pieces were there all along - scattered about, perhaps a few were broken. But now, they returned to their proper place, creating a functioning mechanism. An inner clock, meticulously reconstructed. And now, the machine was slowly turning over - one tiny click at a time.

The piazza was packed with people. And for the first time in this whole trip - I felt among them. Not a wanderer, nor a voyeur witnessing their joy. Today, I was invited to the party. I watched the clouds whiz by the towers, the sun beamed down on my face. That perfect day after a nice rainy storm. Not everyone gets second chances in life - I've been given two or three hundred. And this one wasn't getting past me.

The lever was thrown - the machine was now in full swing - pendulum swinging, well-oiled parts moving furiously.

Life unfolded before me, and I was back in the game. I was fully aware. The man with one eye is king in the land of the blind. I'd rather have both eyes open wide, and be among the masses. And that was today.

I realize - I mean really get that there is no past - and no future. We have now. This second, right here. The past is gone, and is often used to gage what the future would bring.

A yardstick. But now - well, it is what it is, no promises, no compromise - just being what it is in that moment.

And I was **in** *the moment. Kids laughing, people talking. For the first time in my long journey, I wasn't alone. I sat by myself, but I wasn't alone. I didn't wish for the moment to last forever, didn't ask how long it will go on for. Just took it all in. Every second. How many seconds have we been alive, how many do we have left?*

But more importantly - how much time do we spend living in the past, or worrying about predicting the future. And that is what life is about. No more promises. Promises are about the future. Something we don't have - by the time we get it, it's the present. Promises are a way of molding tomorrow based on today. There is no tomorrow.

I realize that people can go as they please, but I also realize that when they stay - it doesn't matter for how long - because in that moment, they choose to be with you - until that moment is over - or until eternity. But every moment that they are with you - it magic. It's that simple - it should be honored and cherished and recognized for what it is: People choosing to share their precious seconds with you. In joy - not hate or fear.

One must always leave the cage open - so that the bird can return. That is how my heart is. Open. People might take pieces and walk away. But I believe that others will return with even larger pieces than the ones that I've lost. It's a risk, a gamble. But one that I now have to take to be truly alive.

As I sat there, I wanted to cry - not out of sadness, but out of happiness. As Yoda told Luke Skywalker, "Never his mind on where he is, hmmm? What he was doing."

Twyla Tharp - the choreographer said - Movement is life - you stop moving, you're dead. That's what I've been focusing on - moving. Because as long as I moved, I was controlling something. Now it was time to stay put, and appreciate where I was. That, my dear friends is the difference between ***living*** *and being* ***alive****.*

Anybody can be born, we don't control that. We all will die - by someone else, our own hand or natural causes. Not really a big deal. But to be alive - that is the quest - the journey. The task put before us. And it doesn't start with broad promises based on our own fear of the future. No, being alive is about now.

Promising to be with someone for eternity - that's just too incredibly big. Nobody really knows what tomorrow will reveal. Every day you open your eyes and somebody is still there - a spouse, lover, or a friend returning a phone call. That's just a miracle. And it's beautiful, real and passionate.

Prague brought that out from me. As I sat there in the square, I felt something sit down next to me. It was the VOICE - the one that told me to go on this whole stupid trip to begin with. And it said - told you it'd be OK, didn't I? Yeah, it was right -- WE were right.

The edge was back, the passion was freed from its bonds. I tried to shake the negative person - lost him in Cologne but bumped into him here and there. But now, he just vanished. And in its place was my angel - heaven sent. It was watching me all along - I just never had the courage to actually see the angel. How often do we not see what is there because we're afraid to look - afraid it might not be what we expect? It's about ACCEPTING not EXPECTING. Expect is about control - accepting is about freedom.

Life - it's not a test, it's not burden or a joy. It's not pain or happiness. Life just is. It happens, don't take things personally. The party here is in full swing. But unlike some people who want to go out with a bang, I want to wait until the music is booming. Sweat is pouring off people's bodies from dancing.

The champagne flowing - and in that moment is when I take my sip of bubbly - blink both eyes and nod, then silently slip away. Like the cool winds of Prague. Nobody noticing, nobody necessarily caring, just drifting away. And without looking to the past, keeping the good in my heart.

I would love to spend another week or month here. Europe is finally in full bloom - both the trees and the life and my heart. But the day is too perfect, the crowds are too passionate - I couldn't ask for a better moment to leave.

The party is at its peak - maybe there will be another peak, who knows? Now is the time to leave Prague - and Europe. I'm ready to go back. To home? Well, what is home - does it matter? Of course not, it's the future, it's tomorrow. And that hasn't been given to me just yet. In the eye of this beholder - life is just grand, vast and limitless.

The time is now - and I'm grateful that it is being doled out to me - every single second. No more wishing away the future, or condemning my past, just playing the game according to the rules of the moment. Although, I realize there are no rules, but the ones we impose on ourselves.

No more compromise - no more promises - no more past to control me. Freedom, sometimes horrible, but always glorious freedom. Freedom from myself and all its mistakes. Freedom to simply be.

Now, I'd be a fool to say that all is well and done. No, I'm just on the right path after going down so many different roads - many with dead ends. The light at the end of the tunnel is no longer an oncoming train. Only a fool would believe such triviality.

It's amazing what I'm able to see, if I'm just brave enough to open my eyes - and let in what is there, instead of hoping to see something that I expect.

But at least I'm no longer leading the blind with my one weak eye. I'm going forward with both eyes open. And not the present - not the past -- but the present is looking great right about now. And the world - well, it's a mighty fine planet, and I'm honored to be back for an extended visit, if it'll let me.

LESSONS OF PRAGUE

To this day, the mention of Prague still makes me swoon. That city will always hold a special place for me as the core of my new being.

The time that people choose to spend with you is precious – every single second. Cherish it, for that particular time will never come by again – for either person. How much time do we spend at work, or sleeping? How much time does that leave each of us to expend at leisure? Not enough.

The people that you choose to spend your time with - do they bring out the best in you? Do you bring out the best in those that you surround yourself with? If the answer to either one of those is "No," then don't see those people anymore.

Do you bring out the best in those that you surround yourself with?

Time is too valuable to waste on people that you don't nurture or that don't nurture you. When I see a bad movie, I feel ripped off because I committed two hours of my life to hear bad storytelling. Same goes for books or TV shows.

If I spend time with someone I don't really like, I'm wasting his time and mine. I have a friend who works 50+ hours a week and is married with two children. Every time we get together for dinner or a drink, I am honored. Yes, honored, that he is with me.

My friend could be with his family, catching up on some R&R, or doing an infinite number of things with his limited time on this planet. Yet, he chooses to spend a block of his time with me. I am not going to waste it. We can still debate, joke or catch up on what we've been doing. We'll even discuss personal problems.

But the goal of our time together is for me to nurture his life. In return, he is nurturing mine, whether or not he realizes this.

I have had friends who I've stopped talking to, simply because our relationships went nowhere. Our interests were different, our goals weren't aligned and we had little to really talk about. By cutting off the friendship, I wasn't wasting their time, nor mine. I freed them up to cultivate other friendships.

When I talk to people on the phone, I am filled with awe. Out of all the creatures on this planet, I have their full attention. It's really an awesome way to view the world.

I also recognize that it is a two way street. I may be perceived as negative or boring by somebody else, which is why he doesn't want to be with me. I have no problem with that. In fact, thank you for not "putting up with me." Now, I can use my time to cultivate new friendships or reinforce my existing ones.

ACCEPT NOT EXPECT

Now is the time to begin **Accepting** and not **Expecting** life to go as smoothly as you would like it. I find that sometimes whatever I'm resisting, keeps existing. Going with the flow allowed magical things to happen.

As an example, my viewing of the Olympic Park in Munich or my hiking trip in the mountains. My side trip to Rothenberg was a completely unexpected treat.

When I tried to control things too much, my plans backfired. My first day in Cologne was a bit rocky. So was my first day in Prague. In both cases, I was trying too hard to get a firm plan for what I was doing for the rest of my journey. When I set my touring strategies aside and simply took in the sights, or enjoyed a beer, my blockage slowly went away.

By accepting my situations, for better or worse, I came out ahead. It was the expectations for a specific outcome that would cause me emotional turmoil. When life isn't going your way, just roll with it.

MAY 2

So here I am in Berlin - quite the city, it reallz has a beat all its own, up there with New York for sure. Pulled in and got tickets for an overnight train to Amsterdam - then I realized that May 1 is a holidaz weekend. What's going on, didn't zou just have Easter?

I walked around, 'cause I onlz had two hours before the train, then decided, nah, let's stick around. Got a hostel, had a room for four all to myself. Not a bad way to end a stellar daz. Returned the ticket - the German ladz behind the desk made some derogatory remark in German.

Just once, I'd love to be fluent in a language, speak in English, then zing them in their own language when they say something out of line. Not reallz a big deal, water off a duck's back.

Near the station is the bombed out shell of a church - huge scars mark the sides where shrapnel tore into it - no stained glass windows, and a part of the steeple is missing. Yeah, they started the war, they paid the price in spades. Everywhere I go, there are still the ghosts of the great tragedy of the 20th centurz. The zounger generation seems to be more peaceful, and determined to bring Europe together, not tear the world apart. Anzwaz, that's been mz observation of Germanz. A peaceful, warm people. Odd, huh? Well, preconceptions will lead zou astraz everz single time.

So, after I left Prague on an incrediblz sunnz daz that had me wanting to staz forever, I witnessed the incredible spectacle of the river beside the tracks. People fishing, camping, enjozing life. That's what I witnessed. Life unfolding before me - mz window to the word, except the world came to me. Nobodz even knew I was watching.

Then, another magical moment. Golden fields of wildflowers, endless plains sweeping to the horizon. And modern windmills, at least 300 feet high, swirled majesticallz, stretching up to the deep blue skz. Clouds drifted overhead - the majestic ships of the air doing their thing. Floating.

And then I cried. Not loud like a babz, but just tears of happiness. I made it. I went through and broke out the other side, and I knew it. Just me, and the movement of the train, had almost the whole car to myself. All of it for me.

Well, mazbe not --- but it sure felt like it, and wow, I was going to give mzself that one.

The car moved back and forth - Clickity Clack - as the wheels glided across the iron road.

And there he was, in the seat next me.

Me.

-- Where have zou been?
...Right here, the whole time.

--- How come I never saw zou.
....Gotta open your eyes to see. Been a long trip?

--- You have no idea.
....Oh, I think I do.

---- So, where are we?
....Germany, just past the Czech border.

--- No, I mean....
.... I know what you mean. The other side. We did it. Feels good, huh? Never doubted you for second.

--- Yeah, it feels like it was forever.
.... It was an eternity.

--- Letting go can be hard.
... Nah, it's holding on too tight that'll kill ya.

--- Gorgeous day, how long do you think it'll last?
... As long as you want it to, then the sun will set, and there'll be another daz.

--- Promise?
.... Never.

--- Good. That's how I want it to be.
... Then so let it be done.

--- I missed you.
... Missed you too, let's stick together from now on, 'K?

--- Promise. <wink> But what're we gonna do when we get back?
... Shhhh! There's another field of flowers on the right that you don't wanna miss!

Clickity Clack Clickity Clack Clickity Clack.......

15

BRACE FOR IMPACT

END GAME

That was it for me. I had burst out of the woods and into the clear. My life wasn't completely roses after that. I still had my share of meltdowns and tough days. But that was it - I had gotten past the worst part of my divorce.

I never had any days that were worse that my numerous low points on that journey. After Prague, my life was on the rebound.

I don't think that a day goes by that I don't think about that train ride. I knew right then and there that everything was going to be OK. I achieved this pinnacle by understanding that I was being very childish.

CHILDISHNESS

How did my trip to Europe make me feel? Humble, for it revealed how ungrateful I had been.

We've all seen parents fussing over their child. They cry and whine and the parents are trying to make things right. First it's holding them, maybe a funny toy, then comes the bribery with ice cream or candy. Through all this, the kid is miserable and making everyone else feel just as bad.

During my journey, I was that child. Fussing and whining about how cruel life was.

I was incapable of realizing that the world was going out of its way to accommodate me and try to bring some happiness to my existence. I was ungrateful.

Everyone I met in Europe told me that the spring was unseasonably warm and rain-free. I was never mugged, nor did I feel in danger for my life. I never had a problem finding economical lodging.

I was ungrateful.

I lost weight because I was doing so much walking. I had time to myself to work through my problems. How many people could take that much time off work?

It wasn't until the end of the trip when I finally realized that I had been totally dismissing all the blessings that the world was offering. That's when I finally came to my senses. I felt that the world was relieved.

It wasn't asking for an apology or an explanation. It just wanted me to be happy. When I acknowledged that happiness, I felt bonded to the world again.

It was as if I was in my room, grounded for something that I did. When I realized my mistake, I was allowed back to the party and all was forgotten.

Enable yourself to forgive yourself. If you can't forgive yourself, than don't expect others to. At some point, you will get tired of hearing yourself complain. Then, your life can make a turn for the better.

THE AVACADO

There are two entities inside you, two separate units of the "Self". You are an avocado.

First, there is the **Core**. It's the center of our beliefs. The danger lurks when it entraps us into thinking only of ourselves in such a way that shuts out any rational thought. When I was in my darkest place, I felt so victimized and blind-sided that I couldn't concentrate on anything else, except my pain. I lived in the core.

There was no way to free myself from those bonds. That created a vicious circle where my victimization became justified. Until I was able to let go of those thoughts, I could never get past such a feedback loop.

The second unit, is the **Rind**. This is the part of the self that interacts with the rest of the world. It's adaptable and open to change. However, this part cannot subsist without drawing its beliefs from the Core.

The best balance is to live in the Rind, but draw from the Core. If you live in the Core, then the Rind will shrivel up and die.

But if you nourish the Rind with the knowledge from the Core, the Core will be forever protected. The Rind is the point where the rubber meets the road.

The Core doesn't see the road, nor should it. It doesn't need daily maintenance, just an occasional cleaning.

MOVING FORWARD WITH THE BUFFET

Americans have always been fascinated with dieting, even more so in recent years. I've traveled to parts of the world where malnutrition is a serious problem. Who would've thought that we would spend millions of dollars a year to combat health ills due to overeating?

It seems unreal that while other people struggle with finding enough calories to sustain their body on a daily basis, we must contend with ways to stop ourselves from eating to death.

One study I read about, talked about how the people who frequent the "All-You-Can-East" buffets tend to put on weight.

Well, that seems logical - there's so much food, that most people gorge themselves. I know, I've put many such restaurants out of business.

That's not the real reason. It's the variety of food. The human body usually tires of a specific food after about the 3rd bite. We get bored and stop eating.

A buffet allows us to sample hundreds of foods with a variety of flavors. Bored of the pasta salad? Have some roast beef. Tired of mashed potatoes? Slurp some fish chowder. Of course, there's always room for dessert! They have Jell-O in twenty different colors.

That's interesting, but what does that have to do with getting through my heartache?

What happened with me as I went through my pain was that I tended to withdraw into myself. It's a common protection mode - a place we go as a last resort. It feels safe and it gives us an opportunity to brood.

But it also creates stagnation. Without the ability to move forward, there can be no healing. We feast on the same emotional diet that quickly goes stale. In short, we feel there is no escape.

I tended to withdraw into myself.

This is the time to enjoy the buffet of life. Tantalize the senses, reach out and see what the world has to offer. It can be done very simply.

TOURIST TIME

Getting out of your daily routine and into some new adventures can jar you out of your despair. You don't necessarily need to hop on a plane to visit another country.

Become a tourist in your own city. Some of you might reply that you live in a small town, with absolutely nothing to do. Sorry, you don't get off that easy. I have two answers for that one.

First, no matter how small a town you live in, there's something you haven't done, or at least haven't done in a long time. America is dotted with historical sites.

While visiting my father in Ohio, I was fascinated with segments of the Erie Canal. The average person might find a watery ditch unappealing, but I saw it as a piece of history that connected me with the present. It inspired me to do some research on it and learn more about the people who built it and what it was actually used for.

OK, so you live in a small town, there's not a person within ten miles of you, and the entire area has been declared a no-history-zone. In fact, all the mountains and trees have been leveled and there's nothing to see or do. I suppose my exercise if futile.

Nice try, because my back-up plan is impervious. After examining the map of the United States, nobody is more than a day's travel from a city. Now, it doesn't necessarily need to be a large one like New York or Chicago. There's plenty of history and things to do in the smaller cities. In fact, I find those places more interesting because they are out of the way, off the beaten path.

My second point is, if you don't live in a city, get to one. Chances are, you have a friend or relative there - see if you can stay with them. Otherwise, get a hotel room for the night, or make it a day trip. You decide.

Before you leave for the city (or if you already live in one), buy a guidebook for tourists. I have one for Los Angeles, and when I'm looking for something to do, I pretend I'm from out of town.

I've been to some great museums, art galleries, and small cafes. These are places that even friends of mine who have lived here for twenty plus years haven't even heard of.

Don't plan your day. Just wander around. Have a target of where you want to go, but enjoy the ride there. There are so many adventures you can get into during the journey.

Take your time. If possible, walk or use public transportation to remove the stress of getting lost while driving, parking or winding up in traffic.

One place that you have to visit, no matter where you go, is a library. I've visited one in almost every city I've ever been to. Each one has its own character and their architecture is unique. I find that the books nurture my soul. Within the walls of a library is knowledge just waiting to be mined. I always enjoyed reading a magazine or flipping through some books while I'm in a strange city.

I can't describe the sensation, but it's like a child finding lost treasures of sights and smells among the hidden valleys of shelving. Who in their right mind goes on vacation, then makes a side trip to a library? Me.

Another place to stop is an old hotel. Every city, large and small, has one that has been around for ages. Taking a trip into the lobby to breathe it in adds a sense of grounding. Imagine all the people that have stayed there over the years. What did they do? Why were they there?

It's like a child finding lost treasures.

I'm betting that just visiting those two places in any given city will open up new adventures for you. It allows you to meet new people and get out of your shell. But this exercise illustrates something even bigger than all that.

You might find the library boring, same for the hotel. What are your choices? You can stay in that place and be miserable, or you can walk out of there under your own power, your free will.

Could this exercise be a metaphor for something bigger that's going on with you? Could it be a way of physically empowering you to stay mobile, while actually suggesting that you have the means to mentally flex your mind to control your destiny? No, it's just a coincidence.

If you feel that you need a bigger conquest, then do a trip out of the country as I did. I needed to get away from the same locations, same friends, and same climate. I needed the change of scenery, a shock to the system.

By stepping out of my safety zone and into completely new territory, both physically and mentally, I forced myself to face new challenges. This took my mind off my own misery.

The trip wasn't simple to pull off. I had to change a great deal of work commitments, secure plane tickets, manage my money and get mentally prepared for the trip. There is one important message I need to impart.

I wasn't prepared for the trip. No matter how well I tried to plan it, I wasn't ready and probably shouldn't have gone.

As I look back on that venture, I'm still not prepared for it! Sounds crazy, doesn't it? To reflect back on that journey and still realize that the timing wasn't right is absurd. But I survived and returned with clarity of purpose and a grounded sense of self.

THE LAST LAST

The last, last; the very last; the final end. This is something that we don't often think about, but I do.

There were many "last times" that I saw somebody who was important in my life. When that time came, did I know that would be the last time? If so, would I have done things differently?

In my neighborhood as a child, I had a close friend who lived two houses down from me. We had sleep-overs, explored the woods around our homes, had tree forts – we were inseparable.

By the time we went to high school, both of us hung around with different friends. Eventually, my best friend became a stranger. We never saw each other, not even in passing.

I can't remember when the last time was that we talked. Did we go on a bike ride or were we watching TV? If either one of us had known it would be our last time together, what would we have done? Would our last time hanging out together have been sentimental or sad?

By not knowing that things would be different, made it much easier to enjoy our friendship to the very end.

I remember the last time I saw my in-laws. My ex-wife and I had a great trip and stayed with them for a month in Europe. They took us to the airport where we said our good-byes before we got on our plane to head home.

I brought an old mountain bike with me on that trip, to leave there. If I used it once a year, then it was worth hauling it some 12,000 miles. What happened to that bike? Is it still underneath its plastic cover waiting to go for a ride? Is it in some landfill? I hope somebody is using it.

I had no idea when I was packing up my bicycle, that it would be the last time I would see it, or my in-laws. How different that parting hug would be if I had known. This is why we don't know the future, because we couldn't handle the knowledge. We have enough problems coping with the past and the present.

We don't know the future, because we couldn't handle the knowledge.

There are TV shows that I was hooked on, only to stop watching them and realize years later that they were cancelled. I had a few favorite restaurants that I visited regularly. But I stopped going, and next time I went by them, something else was there.

Chances are, you can remember every detail about the last time you saw your ex-wife. What day it was, what the weather was like, perhaps the final words. I remember what I was wearing, I can even tell you what time I walked out the door, signaling the end of our marriage.

The difference is, I don't dwell on it, overanalyze it or get sentimental. When I think of the last time I rode my mountain bike, I'm sad that I'll never bike through the hills of Italy.

But I can't let it bring me to a regretful level.

I turn the situation around and focus on the phenomenal memory of whizzing through the countryside on a sunny day with nobody else on the roads, and am filled with joy.

COMPARTMENTALIZE

Allow the past to remain there, so it doesn't infect the present or poison your future. If you have vivid and sad memories about your final days as a husband, you need to compartmentalize them. Find a way for them to exist within you, without it affecting you. This is another way of creating pearls.

I think of my emotional attachments to key events in my life as separate tool drawers. I know that my sockets are in one place and my wrenches are in another. I don't need to open any drawers to confirm this. By keeping them closed, everything is neat and organized if I need to get to it.

Organize your emotional attachments to your memories in this manner. You keep them in your mind, but you don't need to access the emotions when you focus on your memories. This is different than suppressing your emotions. Suppression is when you deny your emotions and your past, and therefore any link between the two.

I have many fond memories of my time with my ex-wife. There were some wonderful moments we shared, and it would serve no purpose to simply push the memories out of my mind.

Allow the past to remain there.

I memories are in my mind. Every so often, I think about one of them, but leave the emotion drawer closed.

I've gotten to the point where I can think about any memory of my ex-wife without feeling sorrow or anger. Instead, I am able to talk about my marriage without bitterness or regret.

When the day comes that you are ready to open a memory, your emotions will still be there. It will be a different experience, because you will be able to control your emotions, without having them control you.

MAY 3

Well Golly, Gee Whiz Wally! Me and Gilbert went for a walk by the train station, and Gilbert blew all our monez on a crooked card game!

Berlin has absolutelz blown mz socks off. What a place. In fact - yes, here comes the bomb - I'd move here in a heartbeat. This place has it all.

Boston - been there. NYC, well, hez, great citz - been there. LA -- Yup, will still probablz be there. Rome is Rome. Milan - except for the Duomo SUCKS. London - not on a bet. Hartford - that'll alwazs be the dream. But Berlin. Theater, culture, architecture, yup. This is it, the citz that speaks to me.

I did a four hour walking tour of the citz. How to describe Berlin - it's the past, present and future rolled into one moment. Todaz's modern buildings are everywhere, but scratch beneath the surface and zou'll find some relic of the past.

Saw the Brandenburg gate where Napoleon marched through on his waz to Moscow, and the Swastika hung until the Russians took 'em down. Saw the Reichstag - Checkpoint Charlie (Charlie is militarz for 'C' --- there was a Checkpoint Alpha, Bravo and Delta) When a group of Americans couldn't get through to East side, the tanks were rolled out on the American side, and likewise on the Russian - tense few hours, fingers on the trigger.

The wall that encircles the citz -- there were manz different walls -- were put up in under 48 hours through some ingenious engineering. The West knew it was going up, and after it did, no US official had anz comment. See, too manz people were fleeing to the West, the East's brain trust, and the West couldn't handle the influx. East took it in the shorts in the political arena, but it reallz benefited the Allies.

The wall was necessarz because at the close of the Second World War, there were about 4 million troops between the Allies and the Russians closing in on the citz. No waz could the two sides even come close to each other for fear of a continued war.

After the wolves on both sides devoured the Nazis (which stand for Nazionalistica Socializma - OK, that's more Italian than German, but that's what it means).

Both sides were afraid that thez'd turn on each other. Thus, the Yalta agreement to cap the citz until a much later time. Well, this created a stalemate that existed until the late 80's.

Berlin was actuallz built bz a few Slavic tribes and the original name has Roman origins which mean Swamp. Everzthing is sandz. The Jews have alwazs been here and the sznagogues that are here are guarded 24 hours a daz bz German Police complete with armored troop carriers.

The police presence sazs 'Go ahead zou loser, pick up that rock and we'll blow zour head off before it leaves zour hand!' No messing around. In fact the German gov't is building and pazing for the Holocaust memorial near the Reichstag. That's like the US pazing for a Vietnam Memorial with the names of the Vietnamese on it -- not an exact parallel, but point made.

The citz is alwazs changing - see, since it was first born, it never was able to make it's own destinz. Rome is Rome, it was born with a destiny. But Berlin is built upon reaction to the different political climates.

I stood on the spot where Hitler's bunker was, and where his charred bodz was found bz the Russians. Nothing there, no monument no marker. Whz? So as not to make it into a shrine. It's just a small grassz park, near some apartments and is covered with dog-poo, how appropriate. Zou stand there, zou'd have no idea what used to be there.

The architecture is verz cutting edge in this town - the old replacing or amplifzing the new. The citz is constantlz reinventing itself. Even our tour guide saw a few things that weren't there 2 weeks before.

It's got a great vibe to it. The people here want to respect the past, remember it, but still move forward. The parliament buildings near the Reichstag are all glass - an open government with nothing to hide, as it propels Germanz --- nee --- Europe into the next centurz.

Saw the place where the books were burned, on a plaque is a quote that said - he who is not afraid to burn books, is not afraid to burn people. There's a huge tower that looks like a rocket ship - it's supposed to - built bz the Soviets as a towering phallus as a tribute to their superior society. There are parts of the wall, and marking in the road of where the wall used to be.

Bullet marks in the buildings and the pavement on the east side remind me that Berlin has been through a lot. I figure, if this city can pick itself up and reinvent itself, then maybe it's time for me to do the same. Architecturallz, thez are rejoining the citz, that was once together, and was torn apart.

It reallz put things that I learned in school in perspective, because I was there seeing it all. Had a good lunch at a cheap place on the east side - will go back there tonight for a ripping partz at a bar. The east side is all the partz stuff, the west is all shopping.

It's almost surreal, words can't describe what is happening here, considering that the wall trulz came down in 1994, when the east government actuallz issued travel visas to its citizens to go anzwhere they want. Yeah, '88 is when it happened, but we're talking complete dismantlement of the whole system.

This was it - the place where two super-powers stood nose to nose. West Berlin was like the hole inside a big communist donut. And that wall went up in the 50's. JFKs speech Ict Bin Ein un Berliner -- well, what that means is that he was a donut. Berliner is a cream filled delight, but everzone knew what he was trzing to saz.

Finallz found a citz that feels like home to me. Or maybe I'm just feeling more connected to the world. Aww Man, I blinked and just missed out on something. Never a dull moment!

16

MISSION COMPLETE

COPING WITH THE FUTURE

Look to the future, eyes on the prize.

Such motivational sayings might be great for your job or if you're an athlete. But for the purpose of getting through this mess, focusing on the end result won't help you.

I used to drive trucks cross-country. There was one spot in Arizona on Interstate 40, just as I crossed over from New Mexico, where I could see a group of mountains called the San Francisco Peaks. On a clear day, they'd be about two hours away. Beautiful, yet so far from where I was. I'd fix my gaze on them, willing them to get closer, or rather, me to get closer to them.

No matter how much I focused, they didn't move, not an inch. In frustration, I gave up. I'd listen to the radio or one of those books on tapes, or watch the scenery whiz by as I cruised – I mean – obeyed the speed limit to the letter of the law.

The next time I looked at the mountains, they'd be so much closer. Now, I never completely ignored the mountains. But it goes to my earlier exercise of keeping what you cannot control on your periphery.

If you can't control it, let it go, and focus on what you can control.

My goal was still out there, but instead of being intensely fixated on it, I appreciated where I was at the moment, and enjoyed it for what it was.

You want to get out of this mess. I really didn't want to be in the place I was in. Whenever I focused on trying to get out, time seemed to stop. We're talking a screeching halt.

Acknowledge your goal, keep it in the back of your mind, and work on what you can control going on around you.

Let's re-examine your Time Web. If you don't have it in front of you, get it. I told you not to throw it away!

ANALYZE YOUR TIME WEB

Look at the segments that connect the events. Are there one or two events in particular that have more segments going to it than any other?

These are your **Fortresses** - your strongholds you can go to when things get tough. It may be a physical place you escape to, or a group of friends you can count on. Whatever it is, it's your foundation, which should be further nourished. No matter what happens in life, this foundation is part of who you are. Retreat there whenever necessary, but don't take it for granted when you don't use it.

Your Time Web has now become your Blueprint.

BLUEPRINT FOR YOUR FORTRESS

The purpose of the Blueprint goes back to our basic planning needs ingrained in all of us. You don't build a house without one.

This blueprint is a roadmap to a new life. Examine the events that seem more isolated, with perhaps only a single segment tying it into the web. Do they need strengthening?

By adding and detracting to the web, you are able to easily examine vulnerabilities in your Fortress.

Be aware that when I use the word Fortress, I am embracing the positive aspects the word entails: strength, security, pride, aesthetic beauty. A Fortress doesn't necessarily mean isolation, immovability, imperviousness or coldness.

Many years ago, someone suggested that I create a secret and happy private space in my mind. Whether it is a fictitious realm or an actual place, this was to be a safe harbor when the seas got rough.

So, I found such a place and imprinted it in my mind. That place was my former in-laws' house in the mountains of Italy.

When my divorce was in its infancy, I found it very difficult to mentally retreat there. I went through so much inner toil when I realized that I may never go there again. So much for my fall-back position!

I decided that the best way to handle this blow to my secret place was to create a more rational system. Ironically, since coming to terms with my divorce, I can actually call upon that mountain haven, without feelings of regret or sorrow.

I realized that my safe place in Italy is still based on my own experience. It has nothing to do with my ex-wife, as her memories of the area are different from mine. I can enjoy those thoughts as much now as I did then.

But during the moments when I needed a fall-back position, I found myself paralyzed. Have your own, unique place that isn't tied to anyone else - thus, the Blueprint.

It's simply a nuts and bolts "how-to" diagram when things get crazy.

When the emotions run too high, having a tangible map of your strengths that you can fall back on saves the day. I still find areas of my life that need polishing up. Other painful areas of my life, I managed to isolate.

This Blueprint should be a living entity that is subject to modifications over time. It's not etched in stone for the remainder of your life, since your personality and emotions will change. Allow it to adapt as you grow.

TIME WITHIN THE MARRIAGE

Hopefully, you've made a great deal of progress in coping with your divorce. I'm confident that you have.

I'm sure this hasn't been an easy journey for you. I know that you're ready to bandage your wounds and launch off in a new direction.

Earlier, we talked about cherishing time with the people around you. If you spend time with somebody else, you shouldn't be wasting his time - just as you don't want people wasting your time, if the relationship is fruitless.

This idea ties into your marriage. You must acknowledge that even if your marriage failed now, you did spend an enormous amount of time with that person. No matter how it ended up, during that segment of your life, your ex-wife chose you over everyone else.

It's that very reason that makes it so cruddy that the marriage is over. It sucks. It tears your heart out. But now you can get past the final hurdle.

Acknowledge that the other person did spend time with you, just as you did with them. But the acknowledgement stops there. Just because you had time together, doesn't guarantee future returns. It works this way in friendships as well.

Most likely, you are looking at the time you two spent together as an investment. Don't even try to argue with me on this one. I'm a guy, it's how we're wired. We put a certain amount in, hoping for a greater return at some point. There's nothing wrong with that angle.

People are free to come and go in life. We are all separate entities, tied to each other only by **choice**.

CHOICE – THE DOUBLE-EDGED SWORD

Choice allows people to flock to you, and also enables them to leave just as quickly. But this is the only, pure way for two people to exist together. What's the alternative? A relationship based on fear and intimidation? That's not what creates love; it will fail sooner or later.

Leave the door open. If it's locked, then people can't escape. But more importantly, new people can't come in.

Hopefully, you're still not thinking, "since we're getting a divorce, this whole marriage was a waste."

Leave the door open.

You may feel justified thinking this. But get ready for this bombshell. You're wrong, so stop thinking that way.

This was the single, hardest thing for me to realize.

It took me even longer to accept. I'm not asking you to absorb it all right now. Just let it simmer in the back of your head.

Let's continue.

NOTHING IS EVER WASTED

Really? You dare question me with a raised eyebrow.
Yes, Really!

Remember the time you were out with your pals, and you waited all night to ask out the hottest girl at the bar only to:

A) Have her throw her drink on you.
B) Stumble over your words so you came across as a complete idiot because you were consuming too much "liquid courage" before approaching her.
C) Get thrown out of the bar by her boyfriend, who was an ex-pro football player now working as the doorman.
D) All of the above.

When it was all said and done, you stumbled home alone, fell asleep in your clothes and woke up with a pounding headache.

Now, was that night a complete waste of time? You probably answered no. Why is that? Because you still had **fun** and you **learned** something.

The same thing goes for your marriage. You two had some great times together and you grew in ways that you probably don't even realize.

If you didn't have any great times together, then why would you be upset that the marriage is over?

Pretty deep, huh?

I can't think of one practical thing I learned in college. There's not a single moment in my life when I've said, "Hey, that sociology class just paid off for me!" College taught me how to learn and process information.

Your marriage taught you how to live with someone of the opposite sex. The conversations you had helped you formulate your opinions and develop you as a human being.

After the night you got shot down at the bar, did you swear off drinking or bar hopping with your friends? If you did, it was because you felt you learned that the life of drinking and bar hopping wasn't what you wanted in life. I have a feeling you went back at least once more, because you were a glutton for punishment.

Guess what? When you get past your pain and sorrow, you'll be open to the possibility of having a relationship again. That's just how life works.

I've seen my share of bad movies. I've even walked out of a few and demanded my money back. But I still love going to the movies, despite those setbacks. I've had bad meals at certain restaurants, but I've never sworn off any genre of food.

Look at your marriage as one bad meal in the menu of life. Are you really going to stop eating? Do you want to cut yourself off emotionally from connecting with another person? Granted, you probably won't get hurt if you cut everyone out of your life, but you won't feel anything either.

Remember what I said in the beginning, no matter how miserable or hopeless you feel, pain reminds you that you are alive. It just gets easier from that point on.

If you think that anything you've done in life is a waste of time, than lock yourself indoors and unplug your phone until you can come out and play nicely with the rest of us.

Pain reminds you that you are alive.

Saying that your marriage was a waste of time belittles everything the two of you worked for. Mostly, it does a disservice to yourself, because you are willing to erase that part of your life and leave a large, gaping void.

Are there any other aspects of your life that you feel were time wasters?

For now, don't pass judgment on the marriage as to whether or not you wasted your time. There's a tad more territory to cover.

MAY 4

Game time people! The clock is ticking -- but then again, hasn't it been all along?

Here I am, after an unusual night out in Berlin - strange city, not unsafe, just different. Enjoyed myself, and rapped with my roommate for a bit, he's from Holland, looking at a school in Berlin.

Got up, we both took the same train back to Amsterdam – he got off at his stop, which was after 4 hours. My trip was right at 6 hours - had a beer in the bar car, napped, but mostly stared out the window. It's amazing, when you gaze out at the trees, fields and houses, how peaceful it is - grooving tunes help.

Soothing - people getting off and on the train. I was the only one in my car who rode the whole way -- Berlin/Amsterdam. Sounds exotic, in a very Nordic sense. Really enjoy the trains - a highlight to all my trips to Europe. Clean, simple and comfortable transportation.

So, time to wrap this baby up - got some Euros, Gold Bullion, Rare Tibetan Necklaces and Monopoly Money burning a hole in my pocket. Out of the hostel early tomorrow morning before 8 am, got a 10:30 flight.

No don't give me that closure line, if I want closure, I'll use the door.

I did notice while listening to my tunes, how many of them were about love. Ahhh, that ethereal element that was the source of so much pain for me. How many times hath love wrought her evil fury on the wicked and chaste alike. (Just made that up, not bad, huh?)

So, what did I learn? Not sure yet, I'm sure I'll be mining lessons learned for years.

What will the future bring me – Don't really care.

What was my favorite part of the trip? No comment.

Do I believe in love? Yes, I do.

But for all its peaks and valleys, high points and low points, well --- the time of your life, huh kid?

POCKET FULL OF NICKELS vs. THE FIVE DOLLAR BILL

With past relationships and current attitudes towards work, I find myself falling into the rut of Nickels vs. The Five Dollar bill.

We all set goals for ourselves in life. At some point we reap our rewards. But when do we decide to cash in our chips? Far too often, I get obsessed with work and I keep my eye on the big prize. I won't take a vacation or even a few days off to enjoy some rest and relaxation.

In essence, I'm letting the Five Dollar Bill burn a hole in my pocket while I slog through life.

Sure, when I eventually pull that bill out of my pocket, I'm a big man on the town. It's living life Broadway style: bright lights, glitter and champagne. But what happens when I'm down to my last dollar, or even fifty cents? Then I know the inevitable is near; I'm about to go through all of the money, then I'll be back to my old routine of trying to save again for my big spending spree.

Now, you're probably wondering what am I'm talking about. Five dollars - has he gone mad? Well, perhaps I have, but just stick with me for a bit.

Now, there's another way you can dole out your reward. You can drop a nickel here and there. Instead of kicking back with the fancy dinners and chauffeured limos (that's right, all on five dollars), I spend it a little bit at a time throughout the year. A small weekend trip every couple of months, a few concerts, maybe I'll just buy some cool, yet useless gadgets.

Instead of waiting for the once-a-year blowout, I try to enjoy some relaxation as I go. I once heard a man describe the European's view of vacation versus an American's.

Europeans would rather spend a month on a canoe, while Americans prefer a weekend on a speedboat.

Now, that may be all well and good advice for the average person, but what does that have to do with your current life situation?

Now is the time to start spending and stop saving. I'm not talking solely about money. Think of that old buddy of yours that's been begging you to go see him for a visit. What about that week-long camping trip you've been planning for years, or that photography class that always conflicts with your work and schedule?

There is no future, and tomorrow will never come.

IT'S NOT SOMEDAY, BUT TODAY

Maybe a friend or family member lives in another city – go visit them. Your work is offering a new training program – do it. If you have vacation time coming, use it, and go somewhere unexpected.

Take up a hobby, get involved with something you're passionate about.

Now is the time to create a new routine. So do it your way, no compromises, no excuses. You may have been dumped on your butt. However, that also means it's an opportunity for a new beginning.

MAY 5

So where am I?

LA, baby! It was an hour flight to Paris, then about 11 to LAX. Actually, made it off the plane and to the airport curb in about half an hour. First one off the plane, through Passport control, my bag was already there - then through customs. Didn't have to suffer through a cavity search, since I was coming in from Paris and not direct from Amsterdam. Oh well, next time.

Met my roommates in Amsterdam on my last night there. Two were from England, their first stop on a 10 week trip. Very cute, one was actually divorced about two years, and guess what - she called it off. Hmmm, surprise, surprise. The other one, I met the next morning as I was packing - from Australia. About 6' 1", blonde hair, a real knock out. We hit it off well, who knows what would've happened, had I hung out. Most likely, NADA!

I'm staying at my friend's house in Marina Del Rey. Had dinner with him and my ex so I could sign the last bit of divorce paperwork. It was strange seeing her, but we had to get the legal stuff done with. By early September, both of us will be free to legally marry again. Not a big rush for me, I can wait.

No way to sum up the trip, ain't even gonna try. Big question now - where do I live? Stay here or move to AZ or back east, or even Germany - I love that Berlin!

No idea just yet, but I gotta start making up my mind - and soon. On the one hand, it is summer here in LA, nice time to hang out. On the other, well, I feel like I'm starting over from ground zero. Decisions.

Either way time to get busy living again. Maybe it's time for me to grow up.......Nah!

TAKE OUT A CLEAN SHEET OF PAPER

By now, you should have an excellent grasp of what you've gone through and where you want to be. Before we go any further, take a moment to congratulate yourself. Seriously.

It's been a long and bumpy road. I will not deny you that. Somewhere along the way, you've found your way out of the forest, and have seen the brilliant light of day.

You have one final task. It was the hardest one for me to perform, and the most necessary. It's time to take a sheet of paper and pen. Yes, I am an avid typist at seventy words per minute and I can't even read my own signature when I sign my checks. However, I find that in this case, writing by hand links your emotions and thoughts better than typing.

So, you've got your supplies and you're ready to write. You need to write a letter to your ex-wife. Settle down!

LETTER TO THE EX

The letter can be a sentence or a novel - this is completely up to you. What you need to acknowledge is what you did to contribute to the divorce. You may feel that you got the short end of the stick. But there are no true victims in life.

Address it to her by name: Dear Jane Doe. Then go on from there. Don't worry about spelling or grammar. Just let it flow and keep writing until you feel you've emptied your soul.

When you're done, sign your name and put it in an envelope. The next step is very important, and I cannot emphasize this enough.

UNDER NO CIRCUMSTANCES SHOULD YOU MAIL THIS LETTER.

Is that clear? Re-read the last paragraph just to make sure you understand it.

Don't address it. Don't even put postage on it. Simply take the letter and put it someplace safe: in your desk, or under your socks in the dresser. Just let the letter ferment for a while.

This last step, I leave in your hands. At some point - a week, but no longer than a month – go back and read the letter. Read it again and again if you have to, and let everything sink in.

The key to this final step is this:

DESTROY THE LETTER.

Burn it, tear it up and swallow it. I'm just kidding on the eating thing. Make sure you get a burn permit if you decide to torch a 500 page letter.

You are not allowed to keep this letter, because it no longer belongs to you.

After writing the letter, you will have purged yourself. Whatever you say in words, will come from a very deep place within you: a reservoir of pain and suffering.

After allowing some time to go by, the rational part of you is able to process and acknowledge what is in that letter. That's why only you will know when you can read it.

After that acceptance is internalized, you are done with it. Nothing good can come from keeping it. By destroying the letter, you are letting go, but most importantly, you are **forgiving yourself**.

Until you forgive yourself, nobody else can forgive you for what you may have done to them.

What you are seeking in regards to your feelings for your ex-wife is **apathy**.

APATHY

You don't want to wish them suffering in their life, but it's not really necessary to be concerned with their well-being either. They are no longer your responsibility.

Apathy is neutral. It's neither hateful nor loving, but a simple acknowledgement that they have a right to live on this planet. Ultimately, it allows you to move forward without them.

HAVE A NICE LIFE

That's it. I have nothing more to say, because I'm a guy and we're not into long good-byes and high drama. I truly hope this book has helped you.

You've been through a long journey. I'm happy you're on the other side, and am honored you allowed me to tag along on this epic voyage. A truly happy person is one who enjoys the scenery, even on the detours.

Good luck to you.

MAY 6

Woke up early this morning, got some bagels before sunrise. Off in the distance, I could hear the rumble of jets taking off, then I could see their sleek, aluminum bodies launching out over the ocean. I'm back in LA, in one piece, but the mind is still wandering elsewhere. With focus and purpose, I'm ready to begin again. But I can't help glancing over my shoulder at the lumbering aircraft.

Where are you off to, mind if I tag along for the ride?

For more information on this book go to:

www.backpackingthroughdivorce.com

or

www.liquidfootprintpublishing.com

Diagrams in this book were created by Bryan Swoboda of Glaucus Productions.

www.glaucus.com

The book cover was created by Richard Black.

www.rblack.org

Order more copies of **Backpacking Through Divorce!**

Fax orders: 310-745-1421

Email: info@backpackingthroughdivorce.com
or
info@liquidfootprintpublishing.com

Postal: Liquid Footprint Publishing
PO Box 1977
Venice CA 90294-1977

Quantity:__________ @ $19.95 each = $____________

Shipping $____________
USA $4.00 for the 1st book, $2.00 ea. additional copy
Int'l $8.00 for the 1st book, $4.00 ea. additional copy

Tax (8.25% for books shipped to California): $____________

TOTAL: $____________

Name:____

Address:____

City:__________________________ State:_____ Zip:_________

Telephone:__________________________

Email:______________________________

Payment: Check
(please allow 10-14 working days for personal checks to clear)

Visa MasterCard Discover Amex

Card Number: ______________________________________

Name on card:____________________ Exp. Date: ________

Signature: ____